Spelling & Grammar

Daily Practice Workbook

20 weeks of fun activities

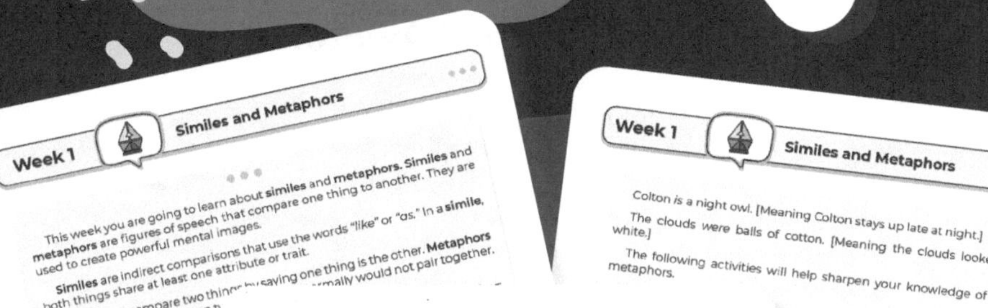

INCLUDES VIDEO

EXPLANATIONS TO EACH QUESTION

TEACHER RECOMMENDED

ArgoPrep is one of the leading providers of supplemental educational products and services. We offer affordable and effective test prep solutions to educators, parents and students. Learning should be fun and easy! To access more resources visit us at www.argoprep.com.

Our goal is to make your life easier, so let us know how we can help you by e-mailing us at: info@argoprep.com.

- ArgoPrep is a recipient of the prestigious **Mom's Choice Award**.
- ArgoPrep also received the 2019 **Seal of Approval** from Homeschool.com for our award-winning workbooks.
- ArgoPrep was awarded the 2019 **National Parenting Products Award**, **Gold Medal Parent's Choice Award** and **the Tillywig Brain Child Award.**

ISBN: 9781962936248

Published by Argo Brothers.

Message from ArgoPrep's Team

In the age of short-form learning, where traditional ***textbooks are becoming obsolete*** *and digital platforms like TikTok capture the imagination, we're excited to offer a fresh, engaging approach to education that aligns with the evolving needs of students.*

At ArgoPrep, we're all about taking learning to the next level. You know how traditional workbooks are kind of the base level for education? Well, we think students deserve more than just the basics.

That's why we've rolled out video explanations for every single problem in our workbooks. It's our way of making sure that no matter how you learn best—by seeing, by listening, or by doing—you're covered. We're tackling the big ol' gap in traditional education tools head-on, making learning not just easier, but way more fun for over a million students across the globe.

Our video explanations are bite-sized to quickly help students get back on track if they are stuck on a problem. This isn't just about getting the right answers; it's about building up those brain muscles to think critically and solve problems on your own. ***More inclusive, more comprehensive, and definitely more tailored to what you need.***

So, here's to making learning something to look forward to, together.

Cheers,
The ArgoPrep Team

SCAN ME

THERE IS A MESSAGE FOR YOU

Table of Contents

How to Use the Book

This workbook is designed to provide extensive practice with the English Language Arts Standards, specifically the Foundational Reading Standard Skills. ArgoPrep's 4th Grade Spelling & Grammar workbook is divided into 20 weeks of content where students will learn a topic followed by various practice exercises and activities.

In 4th grade, students undergo a crucial phase of literacy development, requiring a balanced exposure to both literature and informational texts. These texts serve as tools for enhancing reading comprehension, language development, and knowledge building through various formats like read-alouds, shared readings, and paired readings. By the year's end, 4th graders should proficiently read words and comprehend age-appropriate complex texts.

Our 4th Grade Spelling & Grammar workbook is meticulously crafted to reinforce these foundational literacy skills. It offers a structured approach that aligns with the standards. If you are looking for resources to boost reading comprehension, be sure to check out ArgoPrep's Common Core ELA (English Language Arts) workbook series.

This workbook comes included with detailed video explanations taught by a licensed teacher on our website. We highly recommend watching the accompanying videos as they will emphasize key spelling and grammar principles. Video explanations to your workbook are free.

How to access video explanations?

Go to **argoprep.com/spelling4**
OR scan the QR Code:

WEEK 1

Similes and Metaphors

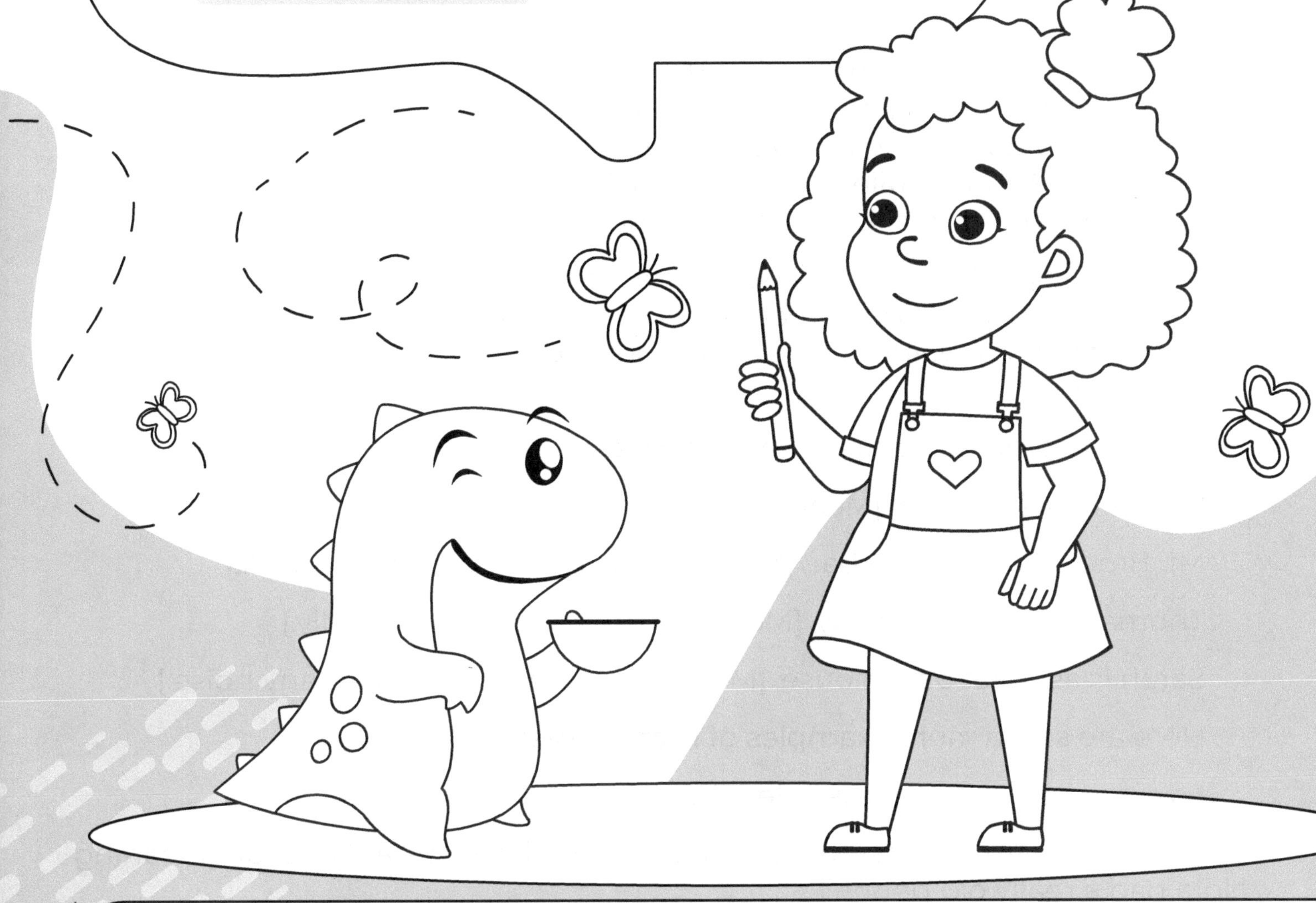

This week, we'll talk about two types of writing that can make your writing more interesting to read — similes and metaphors.

Similes and Metaphors

This week you are going to learn about **similes** and **metaphors. Similes** and **metaphors** are figures of speech that compare one thing to another. They are used to create powerful mental images.

Similes are indirect comparisons that use the words *"like"* or *"as."* In a **simile**, both things share at least one attribute or trait.

Metaphors compare two things by saying one thing is the other. **Metaphors** make a connection between two things that normally would not pair together. Metaphors will never use the words *"like"* or *"as."*

We'll use the following sentence to create both a **simile** and a **metaphor**: *The tall building sat at the end of the street.* In this sentence, the adjective "tall" is used to describe the building. Here is an example of what that same sentence would be using a **simile**: *The building at the end of the street is as tall as a giant.* The **simile** "tall as a giant" paints a more vivid picture of the height of the building than merely describing it as tall.

An example of that same sentence using a **metaphor** would be: *The building at the end of the street is a giant.* As with our simile example, using the **metaphor** "is a giant" paints a stronger mental image than just saying the building is tall.

Here are some more examples of **similes**:

She swims *like* a fish. [Meaning she can swim very well.]

Mr. Brown is blind *as* a bat. [Meaning Mr. Brown cannot see well.]

Thomas sleeps *like* a baby. [Meaning Thomas sleeps soundly.]

Sarah is as quiet *as* a mouse. [Meaning Sarah rarely makes any noise.]

Here are some more examples of **metaphors**:

Love *is* a rose with thorns. [Meaning love can hurt.]

Nora got a new phone because the one she had *was* a dinosaur. [Meaning Nora had a really old phone.]

Colton *is* a night owl. [Meaning Colton stays up late at night.]

The clouds *were* balls of cotton. [Meaning the clouds looked fluffy and white.]

The following activities will help sharpen your knowledge of similes and metaphors.

Similes  Metaphors

Love is a rose with thorns.

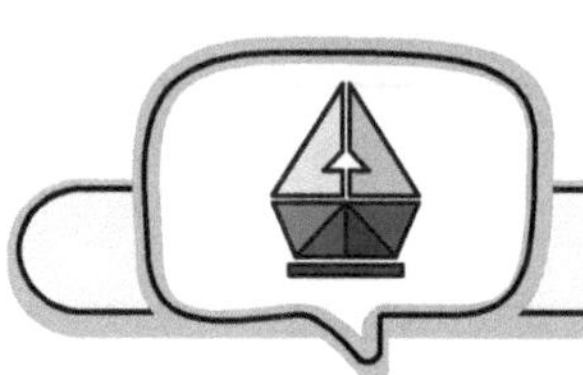

Week 1 • Activity 1

Is it a Simile or a Metaphor?

Directions: In this activity, read the sentence and determine if the comparison is a simile or a metaphor. Write your answer in the space to the left. An example has been done for you.

Example: Simile The blanket was as soft as a kitten's fur.

1. .... He runs like a cheetah.
2. .... He has a heart of gold.
3. .... My grandmother is an angel.
4. .... She is sweet as pie.
5. .... My heart is beating like a drum.
6. .... The stars in the sky sparkle like diamonds.
7. .... The stars in the sky are sparkly diamonds.
8. .... My clothes got wet as water in the rain.
9. .... When I visited Alaska, I was as cold as a snowman.
10. .... You are a dream come true.

Making Sense

Directions: Draw a line between the two things that most closely match in a comparison. An example has been done for you.

Example:

A sweet person	Lion
A courageous person	Sugar

1. Night	An Elephant
2. A Sheet of Paper	A Blanket
3. An Orange	A Tomato
4. A Box of Crayons	A Muddy Pig
5. Something Sharp	An Ice Cube
6. Something Big	The Color Black
7. Something Dirty	Colorful Flowers
8. Something Cold	A Sword
9. Someone Blushing	The Sun
10. Something Cozy	The Color White

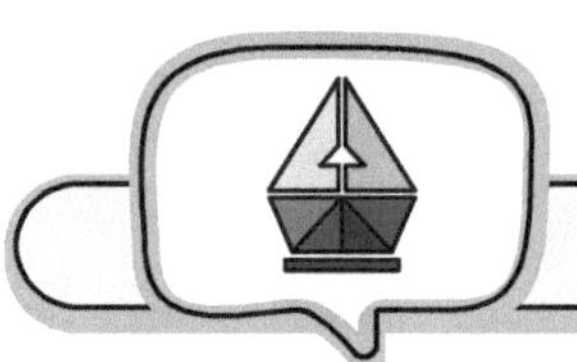

Similes to Metaphors

Directions: Change the following similes to metaphors that convey a similar meaning. An example has been done for you.

Example: "You are as fresh as a daisy," can be changed to a metaphor by saying, "You are a fresh daisy."

1. I ran like the wind.

....

2. The air is cold as ice.

....

3. He eats like a horse.

....

4. He fights like a lion.

....

5. My grandfather's hair is white as snow.

....

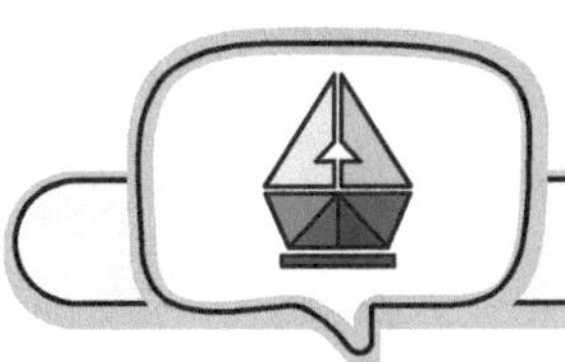

Week 1 • Activity 4

Metaphors to Similes

Directions: Change the metaphors to similes that convey a similar meaning. An example has been done for you.

Example: "The waves were charging horses, crashing on the beach," can be changed to a simile by saying, "The waves were crashing on the beach like charging horses."

1. She is an open book.

   ....

2. Mrs. Norman has a heart of gold.

   ....

3. My best friend's mother is a mama bear.

   ....

4. The pop quiz was a breeze.

   ....

5. You are my sunshine.

   ....

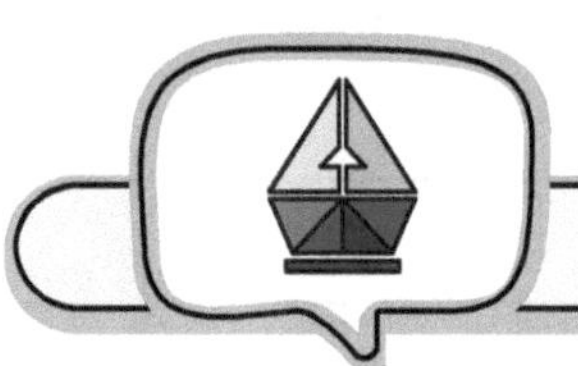

Week 1 • Activity 5

Fill in the Blank with Similes

Directions: In this activity, use your creativity to fill in the blank with an appropriate simile. An example has been done for you.

Example: She works as hard as an ant.

1. Friends are like ....
2. My new puppy is as .... as ....
3. The pine tree is as tall as ....
4. You are pretty like a ....
5. He is mean as a ....
6. The twins are as different as .... and ....
7. Billy can run like ....
8. The knife is sharp as ....
9. Your hands are cold as ....
10. The water is so warm it feels like ....

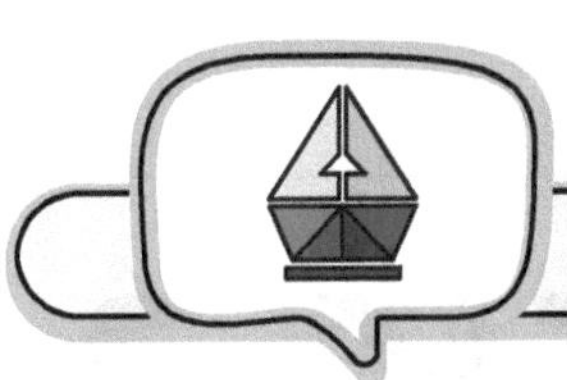

Week 1 • Activity 6

Fill in the Blank with Metaphors

Directions: In this activity, use your creativity to fill in the blank with an appropriate metaphor. An example has been done for you.

Example: <u>My sister is the apple of my eye.</u>

Metaphors:

1. The shadows are ....

2. My love for you is ....

3. Time is ....

4. His voice was ....

5. My emotions are ....

6. The sky is a blue ....

7. This chocolate is ....

8. That car is a ....

9. My home is ....

10. The birds are ....

WEEK 2

Narrative Writing: Narrators and Characters

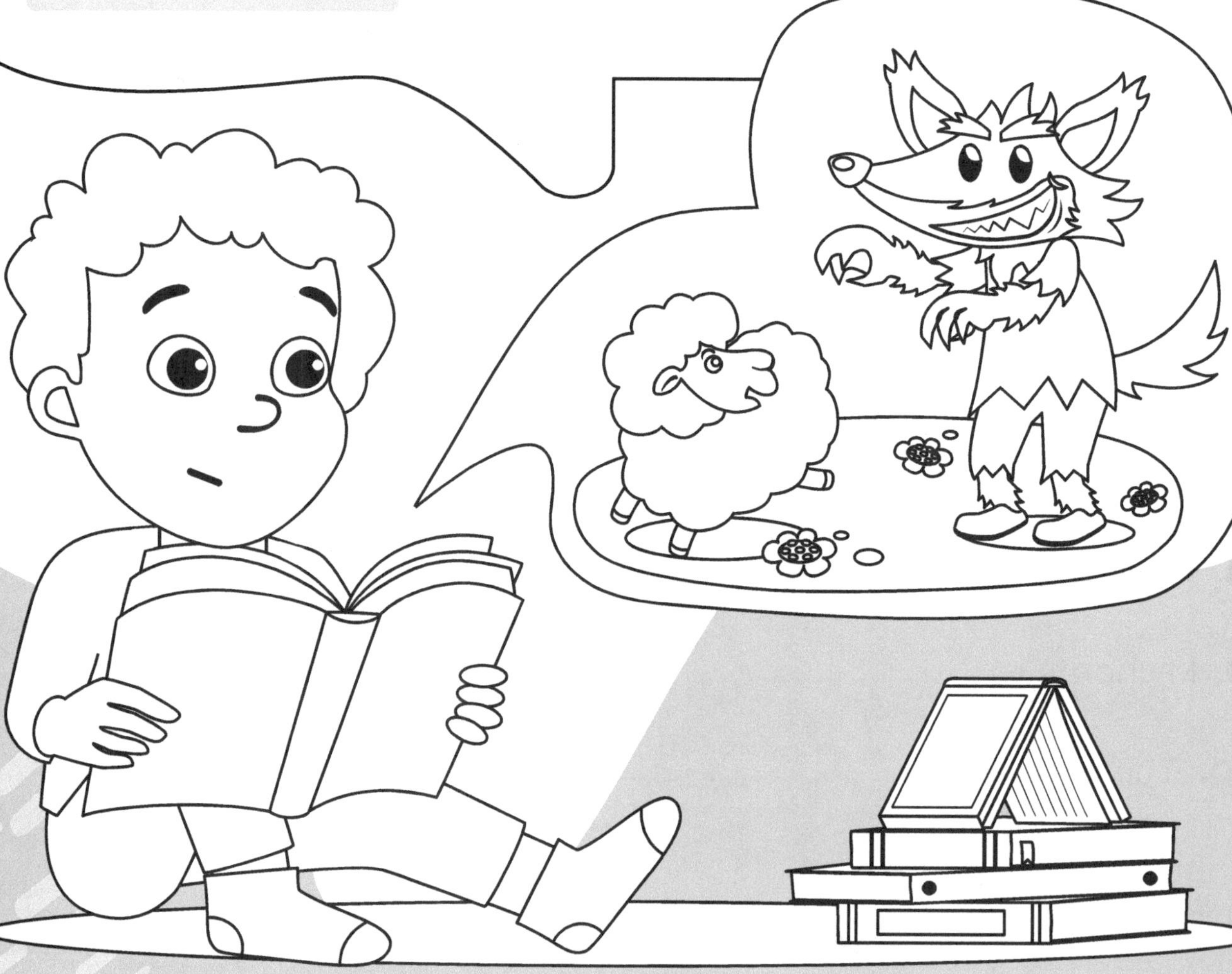

This week, you'll begin learning about narrative writing. Narrative writing is a type of writing that tells a story.

Narrative Writing: Narrators and Characters

This week you are going to learn about **narrators** and **characters** within narrative writing. Narrative writing is writing that tells a story. The story can be either **fiction**, meaning the characters and events in the story are **made up**, or **non-fiction**, meaning the characters and events in the story are **real**.

The **narrator** is the voice that is telling the story. There are three main types of narrators: first-person, second-person, and third-person.

First-person narrators are part of the story. Usually, but not always, they are the main character. First-person narrators will use the pronouns *I* or *we*. They tell the story from their perspective.

Second-person narrators speak directly to the reader. You can identify a second-person narrator by their use of the pronouns *you* and *yours*. They make the reader feel as if they are the main character. This workbook is an example of second-person narration!

Third-person narrators tell the story, but are not part of the story. Third-person narrators will use pronouns like *he*, *she*, *it*, and *they*. These narrators know all of the characters' thoughts and actions and can explain the story from any of their perspectives.

Characters in narrative writing are people, animals, or things in the story that think, feel, or act. While there can be many different types of characters, we'll focus on four major character types that most narratives contain. These **four** character types are: the protagonist, the antagonist, the sidekick, and minor characters.

The **protagonist** is the main character of the story. Most of the action centers on the protagonist. All other characters in the narrative will be there because of some connection they have with the protagonist or action affecting the protagonist.

The **antagonist** is the villain of the story. The antagonist creates obstacles that the protagonist must overcome.

The **sidekick** has a close relationship with the protagonist. This can be one character or multiple characters. They usually help the protagonist by giving valuable advice or helping overcome the obstacles placed by the antagonist.

Minor characters are all of the other characters in the narrative. Their roles are usually minor and the main action and dialogue do not center on them.

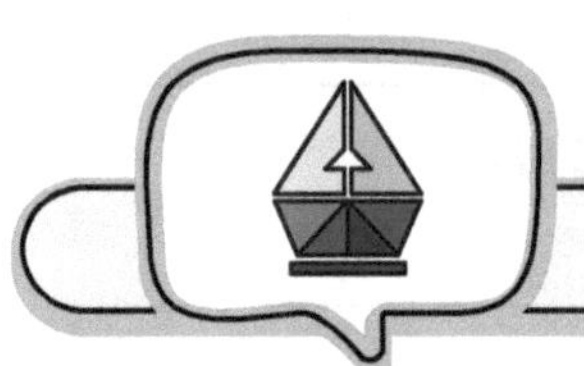

Narrator True or False

Directions: Determine if the following statements about narrators are true or false. In the blank space provided, write **T** for true statements and **F** for false statements. An example has been done for you.

Example: ....F.... Narrators are always the main character in narrative writing.

1. .... There are four main types of narrators in narrative writing.

2. .... First-person narrators are never the main character.

3. .... Second-person narrators speak directly to the reader.

4. .... Third-person narrators know the thoughts of all of the characters.

5. .... First-person narrators tell the story from their perspective.

6. .... Third-person narrators use the pronouns I and we.

7. .... Second-person narrators use the pronouns you and yours.

8. .... Third-person narrators are part of the story.

9. .... This workbook is an example of second-person narration.

10. .... First-person narrators make the reader feel like the main character of the story.

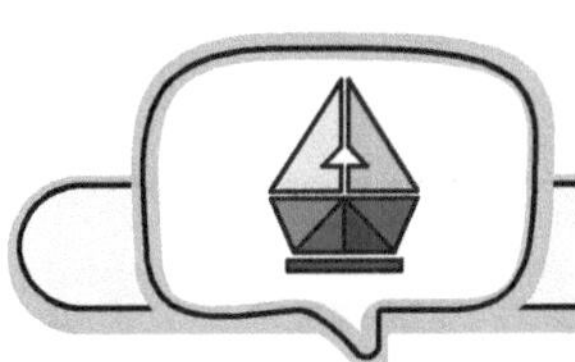

Week 2 • Activity 2

Character True or False

Directions: Determine if the following statements about characters are true or false. In the blank space provided, write **T** for true statements and **F** for false statements. An example has been done for you.

Example: ....F.... There are only four character types.

1. .... Characters are always people.

2. .... The protagonist is the main character.

3. .... The main character's best friend would be an example of a sidekick character.

4. .... Minor characters play a major role in the main action of the narrative.

5. .... A robot can be a character in a narrative story.

6. .... The antagonist is the villain of the story.

7. .... The antagonist helps the protagonist overcome obstacles.

8. .... An animal could never be an antagonist.

9. .... A sidekick might give good advice to the protagonist.

10. .... Minor characters never speak.

Who's Talking?

Directions: Read the following sentences and circle what type of narrative voice is being used. An example has been done for you.

Example: Timmy ran from the well as fast as he could.

First-person Second-person (Third-person)

1. When baking bread, you should never open the oven too early.

   First-person Second-person Third-person

2. Sunny gasped when her mother read the letter.

   First-person Second-person Third-person

3. We never walked home that way again.

   First-person Second-person Third-person

4. The cat slowly stalked her prey.

   First-person Second-person Third-person

5. When you cross the street, always look both ways.

   First-person Second-person Third-person

6. “When you cross the street, always look both ways,” said Mr. Thompson.

First-person   Second-person   Third-person

7. I told them, “When you cross the street, always look both ways.”

First-person   Second-person   Third-person

8. Do you like cheese on your hamburger?

First-person   Second-person   Third-person

9. We should really get started on our homework.

First-person   Second-person   Third-person

10. He hurried home so he could tell his sister what happened at school.

First-person   Second-person   Third-person

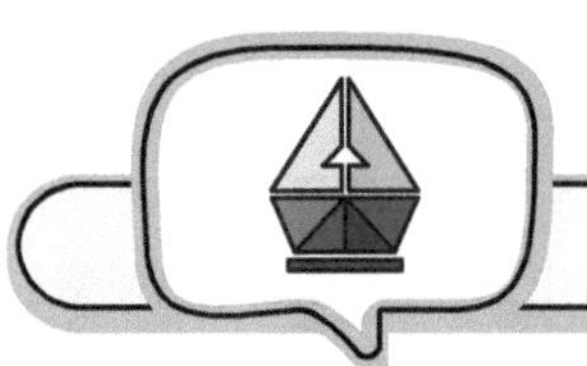

Week 2 • Activity 4

Fill in the Blank

Directions: For this activity, fill in the blank with the appropriate term from the words listed in the box. An example has been done for you.

Example: The ....Hero.... of the story is usually the protagonist.

Second-person	Sidekick
Character	Narrator
Protagonist	Hero
Third-person	Antagonist
Minor	First-person
Villain	Best Friend

1. Most fiction books are written in .... because this gives the author the ability to tell the story from all of the characters' viewpoints.

2. The main character's .... is a good example of a sidekick.

3. The .... is the villain of the story.

4. The .... tells the story.

5. Instructions are usually written in ....

6. .... characters might never interact with the protagonist.

7. A narrative using the pronouns *I* and *we* is written in ....

8. The .... helps the protagonist.

9. The .... is the antagonist of the story.

10. The main character in a story is the ....

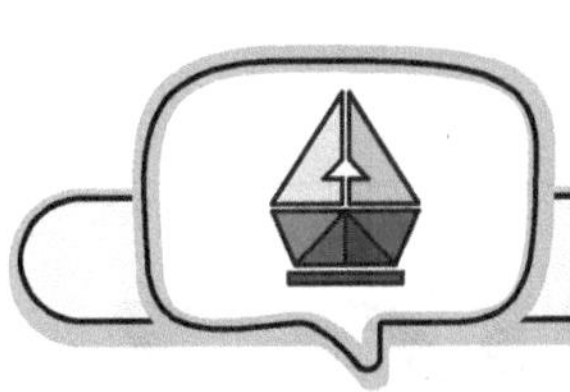

Week 2 • Activity 5

Identifying Parts of the Story

Directions: Think of two of your favorite stories and identify the following key elements. Use a story other than the example given.

Example: Title of the story: *Harry Potter and the Sorcerer's Stone*

Narrative voice used: Third-person

Protagonist: Harry

Antagonist: Voldemort

Sidekick: Ron

Minor Character: Uncle Vernon

1. Title of the story: ....

Narrative voice used: ....

Protagonist: ....

Antagonist: ....

Sidekick: ....

Minor Character: ....

2. Title of the story: ....

Narrative voice used: ....

Protagonist: ....

Antagonist: ....

Sidekick: ....

Minor Character: ....

WEEK 3

Narrative Writing: Dialogue and Descriptions

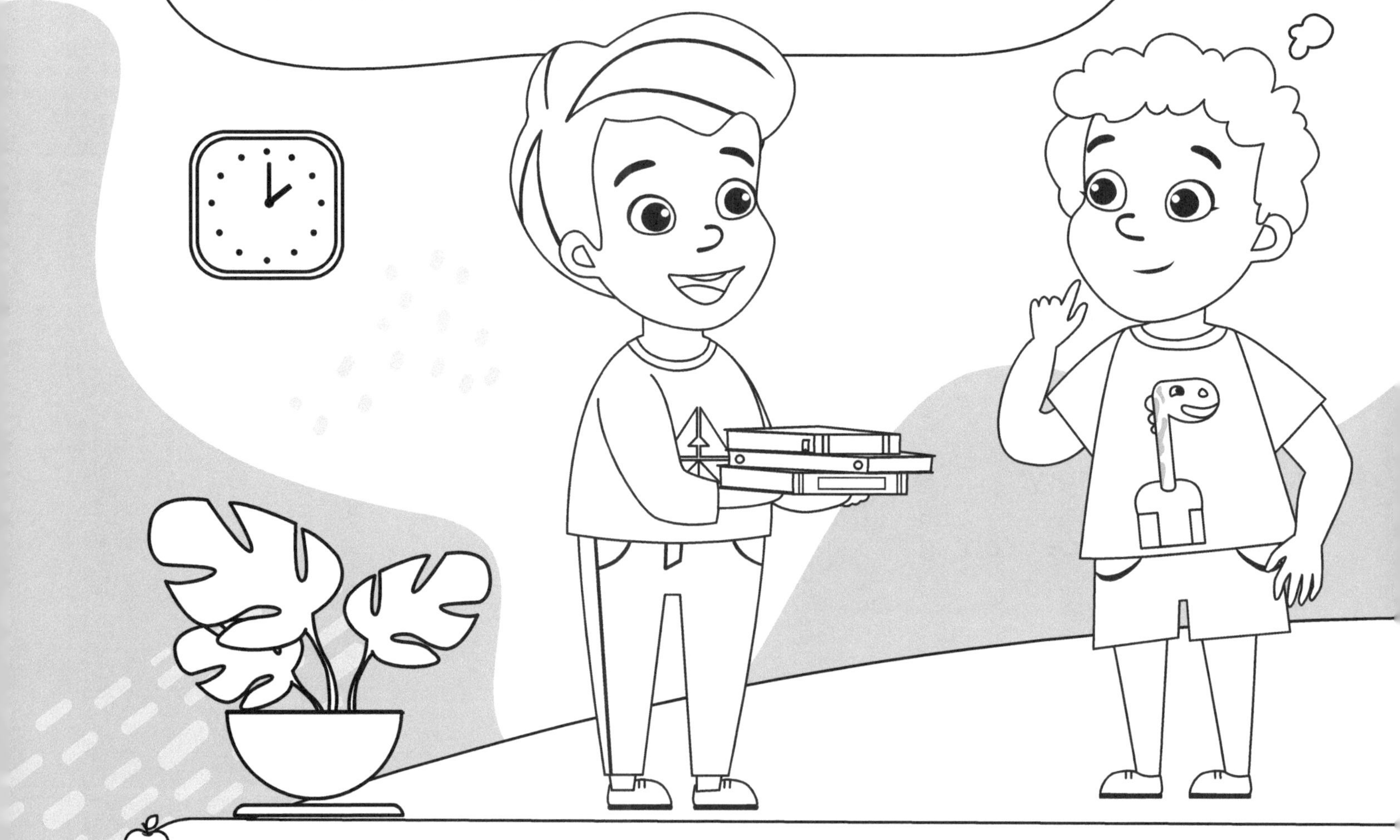

Last week, you learned about characters and narrators in narrative writing. This week, you will learn how to tell your reader more about your story by making the characters talk to one another.

Narrative Writing: Dialogue and Descriptions

This week you are going to learn about **dialogue** and **descriptions** within narrative writing. **Dialogue** and **description** bring narrative writing to life. Both help the reader to picture the story in their mind and understand what is happening.

Dialogue is the exact words a character says. **Dialogue** can serve multiple purposes within a narrative. It can help the reader understand what characters are thinking and feeling. It can also help the reader understand what is happening in the story.

The most important thing you will need to learn to write successful **dialogue** is how to correctly punctuate your **dialogue. Dialogue** is set apart from the rest of the narrative writing by using quotation marks. Here is an example of correctly punctuated **dialogue:**

"Henry, put on your coat before you go outside!" said Aunt Lucy. - Notice that the quotation marks go at the beginning and at the end of what Aunt Lucy says.

The second thing to note is that the punctuation of the sentence being spoken goes inside the quotation marks. You would not write "Henry, put on your coat before you go outside"! The correct way to write the **dialogue** is "Henry, put on your coat before you go outside!" with the exclamation point going inside the quotation marks.

Now let's talk about **dialogue** tags. A **dialogue** tag indicates who the speaker is and can convey the mood of the speaker. In our example above, 'said Aunt Lucy' is our **dialogue** tag. If we wanted to indicate more about the scene, we could write "Henry, put on your coat before you go outside!" whispered Aunt Lucy. Here the reader can understand that Aunt Lucy is trying to be quiet.

A **dialogue** tag isn't always necessary, but they are often helpful for the reader. When the **dialogue** tag follows the sentence being spoken, it starts with a lowercase letter, as in the example above, unless the name of the speaker comes first. A name is always capitalized.

Punctuation in **dialogue** can get tricky, especially with the addition of **dialogue** tags. Sentences that end with an exclamation point or a question mark will keep that punctuation in the dialogue. However, if a sentence would end in a period and is followed by a **dialogue** tag, you will use a comma instead of a period. You would not write "Put the hammer down over there." he said. The correct way to write that sentence is "Put the hammer down over there," he said.

Finally, note that when one character stops speaking and another character starts, this is indicated by a paragraph break. Here is an example where we have the characters Todd and Brad speaking to each other:

"I wish we could go to the movies today," Todd sighed. He knew Brad was grounded, but surely his mother would let him go see the new Marvel movie.

"There's no way my mother is letting me out of the house!" exclaimed Brad.

Now let's talk about **description** in narrative writing. **Description** is a writing technique that brings to life everything in the story that isn't **dialogue**. Think of **description** as a way to make the reader experience the story with all of their five senses. **Descriptions** help the reader to visualize the story in their mind. Let's talk about four ways you can incorporate **description** in your writing that will make an impact.

First, you will want to use words that create vivid details. These words include adjectives, similes and metaphors. You learned about similes and metaphors in Week One of this handbook! Adjectives are words that describe a noun. Instead of writing 'the coat,' you can help your reader better picture the coat by writing "the red coat." Be sure to incorporate all of the senses throughout your story.

One way to help you write more descriptively is by writing out character descriptions before you begin. Character descriptions will not be used in your story, but they will help you establish the story in your own imagination and that will help you to do the same for your reader. The way to create character descriptions is to write down everything you can think of to describe a character. What color of hair do they have? What color of eyes? How tall are they? What does their voice sound like? What do they smell like? How do they walk? Be as descriptive as possible.

Another way to use **description** is to use the point-of-view of a character. As you write, describe to the reader what the character sees, hears, tastes,

feels, etc. Let's say your character is walking down the street. Not everything will catch your character's attention, but they might notice how the garbage truck runs through a pool of water and splashes the sidewalk. Your character will not notice every detail about the people walking past them, but they might take note of the woman wearing the same red felt hat that their mother used to own.

Finally, remember it is OK to let the reader come up with some description on their own. You don't want to overwhelm your story with so much description that it takes away from the action. Instead of describing every detail, leave some things to the reader's imagination. For instance, you would not need to write "the puppy had blue eyes, a long black tail, a white spot on his hind leg, two perky ears, speckled fur, and smelled like he'd just had a bath." Instead, pick out a few things that are important to your story and leave the rest to the reader's imagination. You could write "the speckled puppy had a long black tail and smelled like he just came out of the bath."

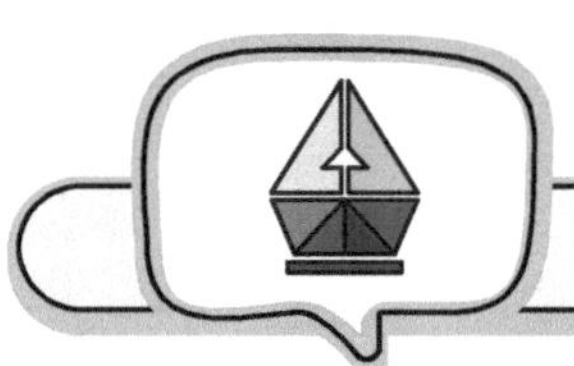

Week 3 • Activity 1

True or False

Directions: Determine if the following statements about dialogue and description are true or false. In the blank space provided, write **T** for true statements and **F** for false statements. An example has been done for you.

Example: ...F... Dialogue and description bring stories to life.

1. .... Dialogue tags tell the reader who is speaking.
2. .... Too much description can be overwhelming.
3. .... Punctuation marks should never go inside of quotation marks.
4. .... Similes are good to use for descriptions.
5. .... It isn't necessary to describe scents to the reader.
6. .... Commas are never used when writing dialogue.
7. .... Telling a story from a character's point-of-view is a good way to be descriptive.
8. .... Dialogue is the exact words a character says.
9. .... Character descriptions are helpful for the writer.
10. .... Descriptions and dialogue are the same thing.

Week 3 • Activity 2

Write It Right

Directions: In the following activity, you will be given two options. Circle the best option. An example has been done for you.

Example:

A. “Stop touching me,” Brad shouted.

B. “Stop touching me!” Brad shouted.

1. A. Paul should not have said that,” explained Miss Ross.

B. “Paul should not have said that,” explained Miss Ross.

2. A. “Simon is a monster”! cried Greg.

B. “Simon is a monster!” cried Greg.

3. A. “Never leave the baby unattended,” said Julie.

B. “Never leave the baby unattended.” said Julie.

4. A. “What do you think the answer is?” He asked.

B. “What do you think the answer is?” he asked.

5. A. She said, “Do you want to go home?”

“Yes,” he replied.

B. She said, “Do you want to go home?” “Yes,” he replied.

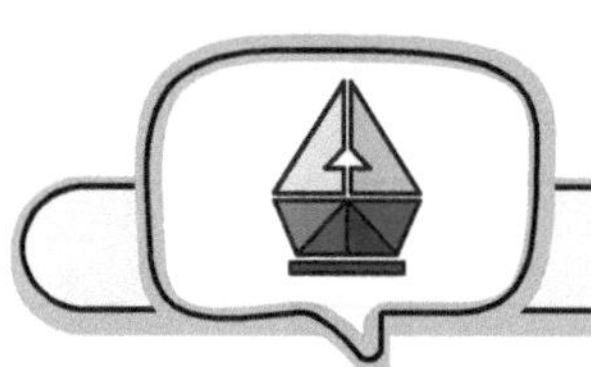

Week 3 • Activity 3

Directions: Read the following excerpt from *Harry Potter and the Sorcerer's Stone* by J.K. Rowling. Circle the ten mistakes. An example has been done for you.

Example: "Is it true?" he said. "They're saying all down the train that Harry Potter's in this compartment. So it's you, is it?“

He turned back to Harry. "You'll soon find out some wizarding families are much better than others, Potter. You don't want to go making friends with the wrong sort. I can help you there.'

He held out his hand to shake Harry's, but Harry didn't take it.

I think I can tell who the wrong sort are for myself, thanks, he said coolly.

Draco Malfoy didn't go red, but a pink tinge appeared in his pale cheeks.

"I'd be careful if I were you, Potter." he said slowly. "Unless you're a bit politer you'll go the same way as your parents. They didn't know what was good for them, either. You hang around with riffraff like the Weasleys and that Hagrid, and it'll rub off" on you.

Both Harry and Ron stood up.

Say that again," ron said, his face as red as his hair. "Oh, you're going to fight us, are you?" Malfoy sneered.

"Unless you get out now," said Harry, more bravely than he felt, because Crabbe and Goyle were a lot bigger than him or Ron.

"But we don't feel like leaving, do we, boys? We've eaten all our food and you still seem to have some".

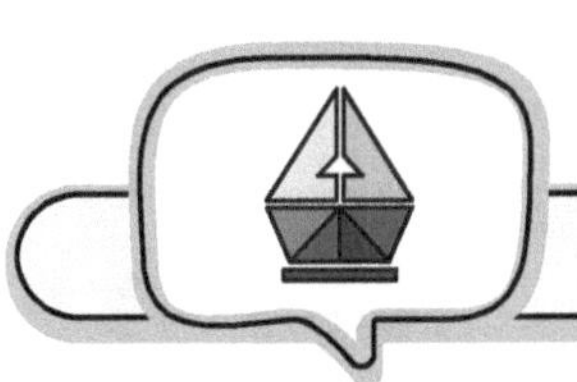

Week 3 • Activity 4

Character Description

Directions: For this activity, you will write your own character description. Be as descriptive as possible. Be sure to include at least ten descriptors. The story is about a mission to outer space. An example has been given for you.

Example:

Character: Spiffy the cat

Character Description: Spiffy is a nine year-old cat. He is ornery and hates to get out from under his blue blanket in the mornings. Spiffy is not at all happy about taking a trip to space and lets everyone know with his constant, high-pitched screeches. When he screeches, his breath emits the foul odor of stale tuna, his favorite snack. However, Spiffy has a very high IQ and is just the cat for the job. When he isn't cleaning his long, soft fur, he's busy doing calculus problems just for fun.

Character: Spiffy's sidekick, Robo the robot.

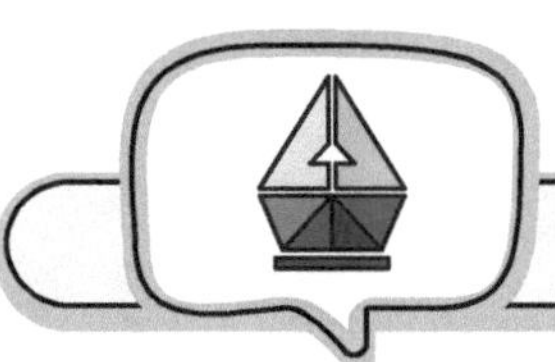

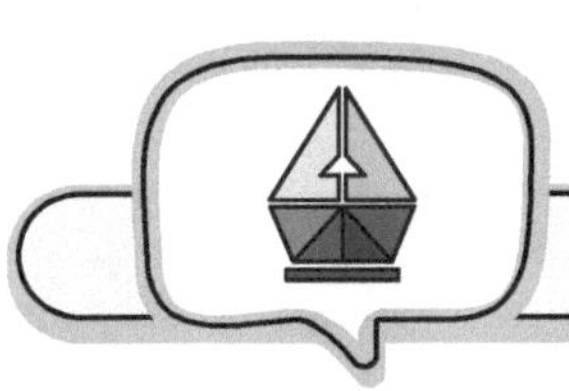

Putting It All Together

Directions: Now it's time to get creative. Use what you've learned in this chapter to continue the scene in the next example. Continue the dialogue between Spiffy and Robo. Make sure they each speak at least three times. Be sure to add descriptions to your scene and pay close attention to punctuation.

Example:

"Spiffy, rise and shine!" Robo exclaimed as he pulled Spiffy's favorite blue blanket off of him.

The cold air immediately hit Spiffy's fur, sending a chill from his white whiskers to the black tip on his tail. "Are you crazy?" Spiffy yelped.

"Not at all. It is five a.m. The space shuttle will be leaving in three hours, and you still need to eat breakfast and pack."

"I told you I don't want to go on this mission," Spiffy snarled. "Can't you go by yourself?"

Robo sighed. He had been up for hours polishing his steel to a high shine, while Spiffy looked, and smelled, like he had spent the night in a dumpster.

Now it's your turn! Finish the scene.

WEEK 4

Word Choice: Emotion

Connotative usage

Emotion

Denotative usage

Word Choice

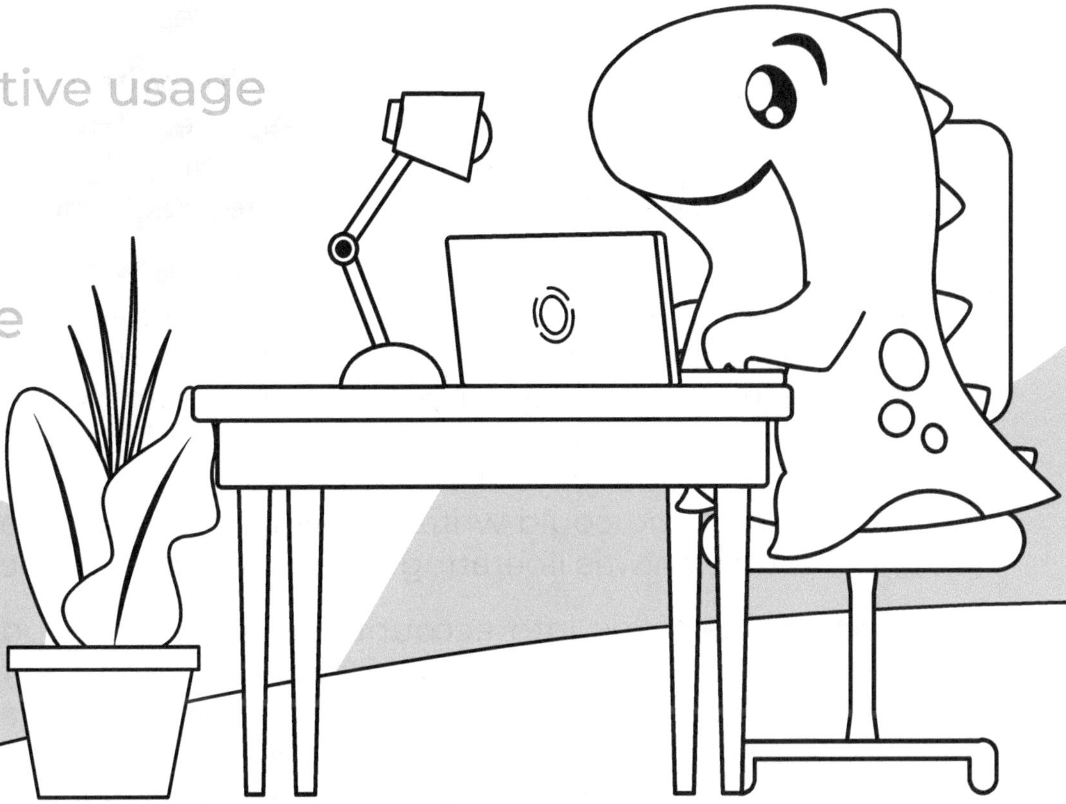

So far, you've learned a lot about narrative writing, but choosing the right words is important! This week, you'll learn how to choose the best words to tell the story you want to tell.

Now that you have learned about similes and metaphors, narrators and dialogue, and the importance of characters and descriptions, it's time to focus on **word choice**. Specifically, we will be looking at words that convey **emotion**.

Word choice can set you apart as a writer. Good writers know that **word choice** is important to help readers fully comprehend and understand the story and characters. When writing, you want to paint the clearest picture possible for the reader, and **word choice** is the way to achieve this.

Word choice conveys meaning. There are two types of usages — denotative and connotative. Denotative usage is a word's basic, dictionary definition and usage. Connotative usage is how the word is being used in a given context. Here's an example of the same word being used both ways:

Susan tells Lexi that she can go shopping with her on Saturday. "That's great!" says Lexi. [Lexi is using the word 'great' in a denotative matter. She uses the literal meaning of the word 'great' to express her excitement.]

Susan tells Lexi that she can't go shopping with her on Saturday because she is grounded. "Oh that's just great!" says Lexi. [Here Lexi is using the word 'great' in a connotative manner. She doesn't literally think it is great that Lexi can't go; on the contrary, she thinks it is the exact opposite of great, and uses the word sarcastically to express her feelings.]

Word choice creates specificity. Specificity is the use of words that are both correct in meaning and specific in description. This is particularly important when choosing between synonyms. Synonyms are words that mean the same thing. However, many synonyms have subtle differences in meaning that are important to consider in your writing. Take for example the synonyms "good" and "liberating." You could write, "Leaving detention was good!" but writing, "Leaving detention was liberating!" implies not just good, but freeing.

Word choice takes into account the audience. Good writers know who their audience is and writes to that audience. When identifying your audience, you want to consider things such as the age of your audience, the setting your work will be read in, and where your audience is most likely located geographically. For example, you might use words such as "wonky" and "goofy" when describing the circus to your friends, but you wouldn't use these words in a legal document read in a courtroom.

Finally, remember that the best weapon you can have in your arsenal when it comes to **word choice** is a wide vocabulary. The simplest and best way to expand your vocabulary is to read! Read what interests you. You may like science fiction, or comic books, or romance. It doesn't matter as long as you are reading. Of course, to really expand your vocabulary, you should also try new genres. You might just find your next favorite author and the perfect word to put into your own narrative.

There are also many places on the internet to help you build your vocabulary. Dictionary.com has a new word-of-the-day every day. Vocabulary.com has a variety of games that you can play to broaden your vocabulary. Merriam-webster.com has vocabulary quizzes that you can take to see how your vocabulary is growing.

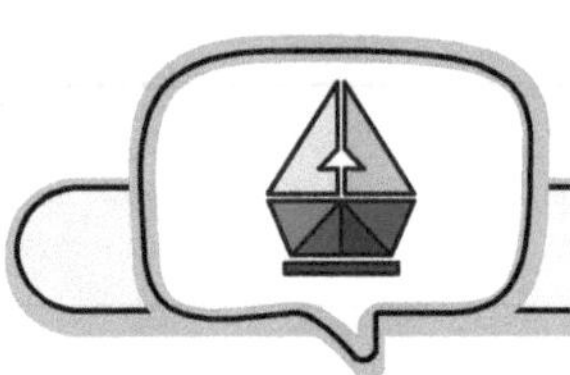

Week 4 • Activity 1

Fill in the Blank

Directions: Fill in the blank for each sentence with the correct word from what you just learned. An example has been done for you.

Example: Good writers consider such things as the age and geographical location of their ....audience.... .

1. .... helps readers fully understand the story and characters.
2. .... .com is a website with vocabulary games.
3. .... usage is using a word's literal dictionary definition.
4. .... is the use of words that are both correct in meaning and usage.
5. .... are words that can mean the same thing.
6. .... .com is a website that has vocabulary quizzes.
7. The best way to expand your vocabulary is by ....
8. .... usage is how a word is used in context.
9. .... .com is a website featuring a word-of-the-day.
10. The .... your work will be read in is important to consider when choosing your words.

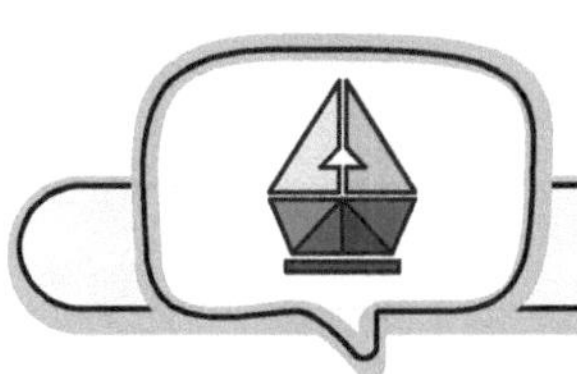

Week 4 • Activity 2

Rank the Words

Directions: Take each set of three words and rank them by the ones that convey mild emotion to the most extreme emotion. Put a 1 by the mild emotion, a 2 by the moderate emotion and a 3 by the extreme emotion. An example has been done for you.

Example:

....3.... Worship	....1.... Like	....2.... Adore

1.	.... Sad	.... Miserable	.... Unhappy
2.	.... Angry	.... Mad	.... Furious
3.	.... Acidic	.... Tart	.... Sour
4.	.... Alone	.... Isolated	.... Outcast
5.	.... Content	.... Jubilant	.... Cheerful
6.	.... Loathe	.... Hate	.... Dislike
7.	.... Hysterical	.... Hilarious	.... Amusing
8.	.... Disinterested	.... Bored	.... Fatigued
9.	.... Uneasiness	.... Anguish	.... Worry
10.	.... Sleepy	.... Tired	.... Lethargic

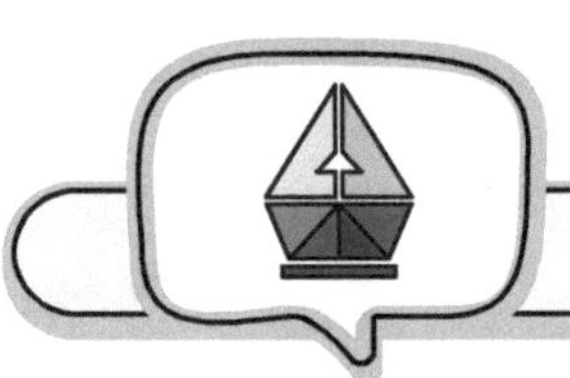

Week 4 • Activity 3

Create a Mood

Directions: Rewrite each sentence below and change the mood of the sentence to the mood indicated. An example has been done for you.

Example:

A diamond ring

Make it convey jealousy.

The diamond ring my ex gave his new girlfriend is big, but it looks fake if you ask me.

1. A missed phone call
   Make it convey anger.

2. Old shoes
   Make it convey sadness.

3. A dog running
   Make it convey fear.

4. A cloudy day
   Make it convey sorrow.

5. A loose button
Make it convey loneliness.

6. An open book
Make it convey longing.

7. A Christmas sweater
Make it convey joy.

8. A cat collar
Make it convey love.

9. An interrupted dream
Make it convey panic.

10. A crumpled piece of paper
Make it convey frustration.

Using Synonyms Correctly

Directions: In the following activity, you will be given a mood. First, write at least five synonyms that evoke that mood. Be sure that your synonyms match both the meaning of the given word and the mood. Then write a sentence using one or more of the words you listed. An example has been done for you.

Example:

Mood: Uncertain

Words to Evoke the Mood: flighty, wavering, unsure, waffling, doubtful

Sentence: Maybe tomorrow the lab results will be back, but I'm doubtful.

1. Mood: Daring

   Words to Evoke the Mood:

Sentence:

2. Mood: Angry

   Words to Evoke the Mood:

Sentence:

3. Mood: Exhausted
Words to Evoke the Mood:

Sentence:

4. Mood: Loving
Words to Evoke the Mood:

Sentence:

5. Mood: Energetic
Words to Evoke the Mood:

Sentence:

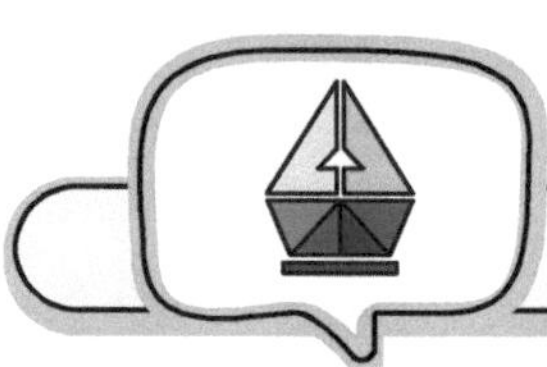

6. Mood: Worried

Words to Evoke the Mood:

Sentence:

7. Mood: Hopeful

Words to Evoke the Mood

Sentence:

8. Mood: Caring

Words to Evoke the Mood:

Sentence:

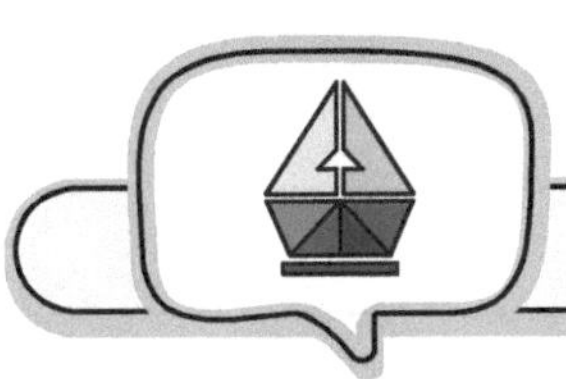

9. Mood: Wishful

Words to Evoke the Mood:

....

....

Sentence:

....

....

....

10. Mood: Arrogant

Words to Evoke the Mood:

....

....

Sentence:

....

....

....

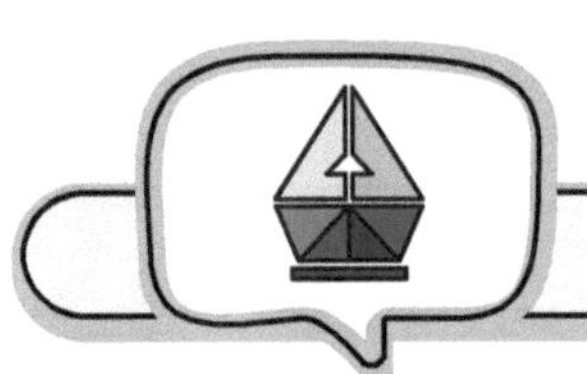

Denotative Versus Connotative

Directions: Read the sentences below and determine if the underlined word is being used denotatively or connotatively. Write your answer in the space provided. An example has been done for you.

Example: She gave him an icy glare after he insulted her writing.

Connotative

1. I fell in love the moment I saw him. ....

2. He fell to the ground when the ball hit his knee. ....

3. In a pinch, you can substitute vegetable oil for butter. ....

4. The baby was so cute she couldn't help but pinch his cheeks.

   ....

5. This silk comes from a remote region in China. ....

6. Her voice sounds like silk when she sings. ....

7. The painting was a lovely mixture of yellow and blue. ....

8. I always feel blue after the holidays are over. ....

9. The groom swept the bride off of her feet before carrying her over the threshold. ....

10. Grandpa swept the kitchen before he mopped. ....

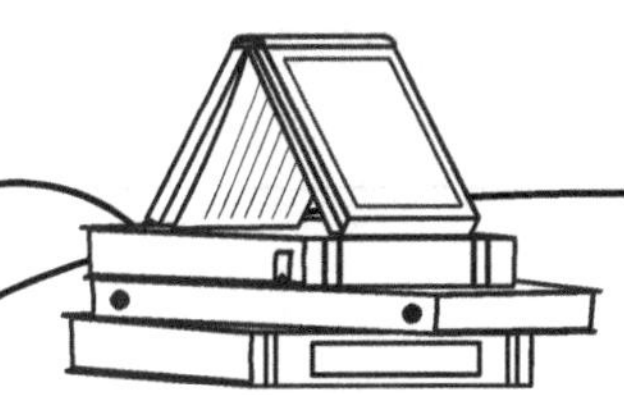

WEEK 5

Narrative Writing: Transitional and Concrete Words

This week is all about tying your writing together! You'll learn how to connect paragraphs together with transitional words and help your readers understand your writing with concrete words.

Week 5

Narrative Writing: Transitional and Concrete Words

This week you are going to learn about **transitional** and **concrete words.** These are different types of words that will help the reader more fully understand the narrative and the characters.

Transitional words help to tie ideas together and can improve the flow of your writing. **Transitional words** may be a single word, but they can also be a word phrase, like "for example." **Transitional words** can generally be grouped into five categories. These categories include time, location, addition, compare and contrast, and cause and effect. Below is a chart listing some examples of **transitional words** in each of these five categories.

Time	Location	Addition	Compare and Contrast	Cause and Effect
First	Above	In addition	Likewise	Consequently
Soon	Below	Begin	However	Therefore
While	Over	Also	Similarly	Since
Next	Against	For example	On the other hand	As a result
Finally	Down	Moreover	Yet	Because

This is by no means a comprehensive chart of all **transitional words** or the different categories **transitional words** can fall under. Rather, it is intended to give you examples of what **transitional words** are and how they can be used.

Now let's talk about **concrete words** and how they help your writing. **Concrete words** describe real things, things you can point to or experience with your five senses. **Concrete words** give readers a clear understanding of the narrative by providing precise details and specific information.

Concrete words can help you avoid being vague in your writing. Here is an example of a vague sentence:

Vague: I basically failed the class for a couple of reasons.

This sentence leaves the reader with a lot of questions. Which class did the writer fail? Why did the writer fail the class?

Here is the sentence rewritten using **concrete words:**

Concrete: I failed Math class because I never did my homework and did not study for the final exam.

Now the reader knows which class was failed and for what reasons.

Keep in mind that **concrete words** often appeal to the five senses, so don't forget to describe to your readers how things look, feel, sound, smell, and taste! To understand **concrete words**, it's important to know their opposite - abstract words. Abstract words describe feelings and things that are intangible such as thoughts and ideas.

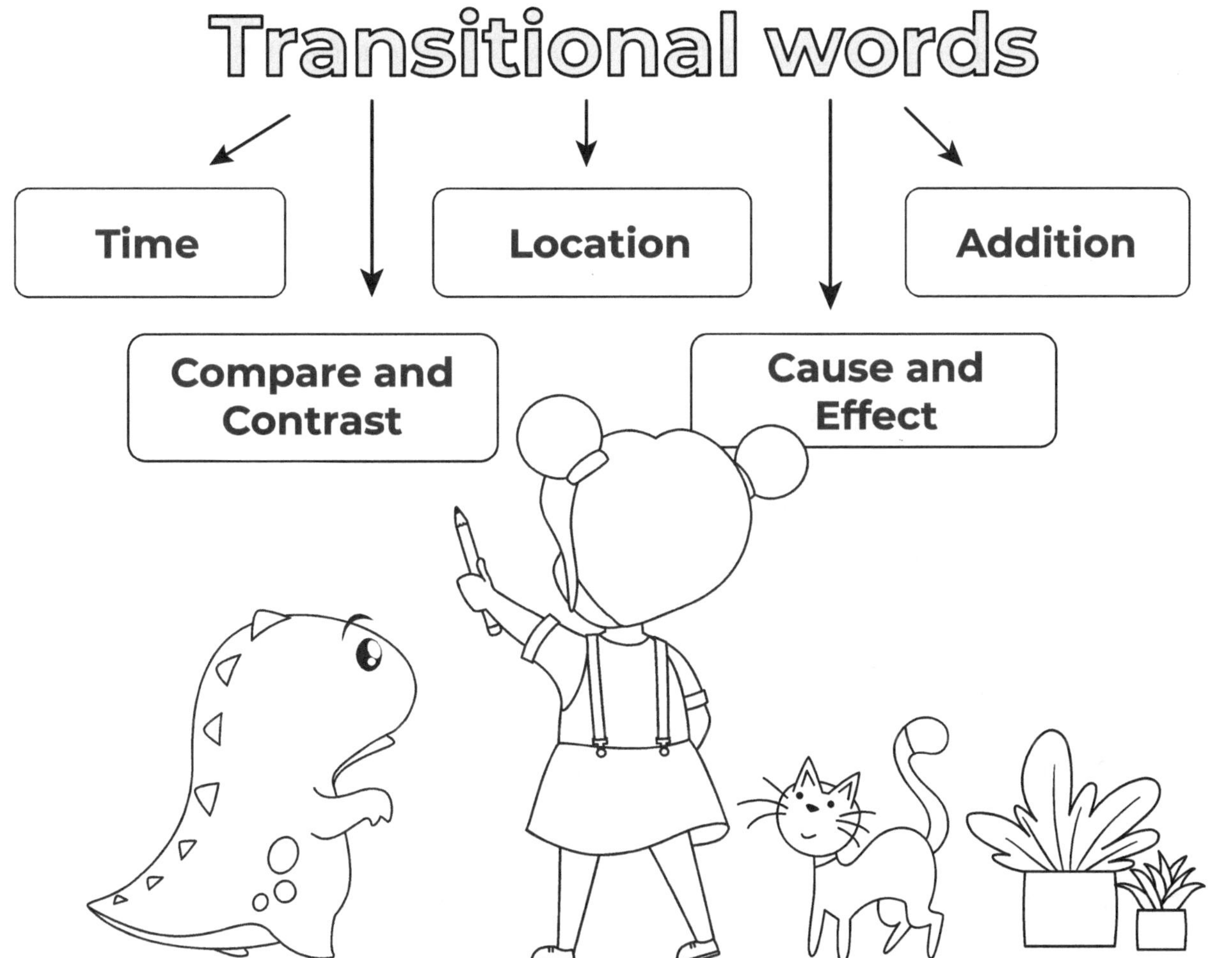

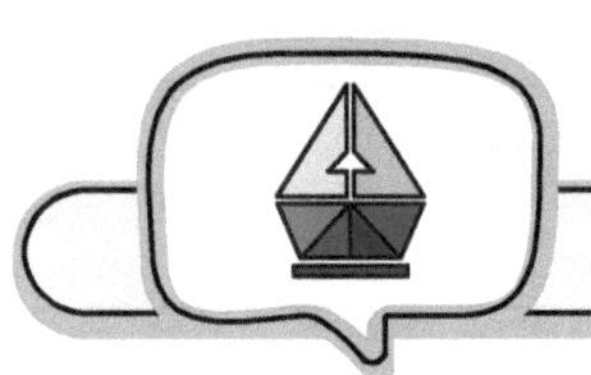

Week 5 • Activity 1

Choosing a Good Transition

Directions: Read the sentences below and fill in the blanks with the best transition word or phrase for the context. Use the words located in the box. Note that no word or phrase will be used more than once and some of the words or phrases will not be used at all! An example has been done for you.

Example: Mary turned two. ....However,.... she was sick and so we had to cancel the party.

As a result	First
Finally	In addition to
Consequently	Down
Because	Meanwhile
On the other hand	Nevertheless
However	Next
For example	Above all

1. .... taking ballet, I also take guitar lessons.
2. Alex finished his homework early. .... , he had time to play video games before bed.
3. I was hoping to get a hamburger. .... , my brother was imagining a big bowl of spaghetti.
4. We decided to go to the park instead of the movies .... it was a pretty day.
5. When making a banana spilt, first peel the banana. .... , slice the banana down the middle.
6. My mother struggled to finish reading her book tonight. .... , she found it difficult to see after the power went out.

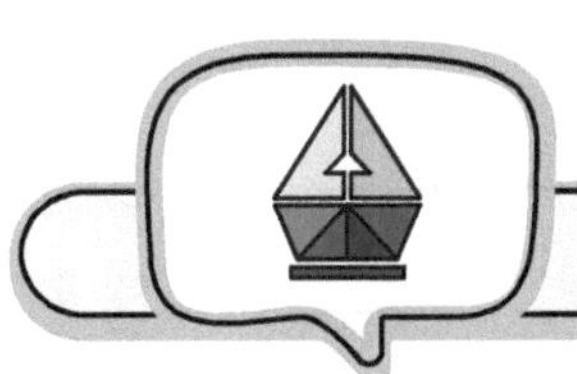

7. There are many reasons you should check the weather before leaving the house. ...., if it's raining, you'll want to have an umbrella with you.

8. I stayed up all night. ...., I fell asleep at my sister's recital.

9. ...., I always start the day by doing my stretches. Then, I have breakfast.

10. We could go swimming. ...., we could go fishing.

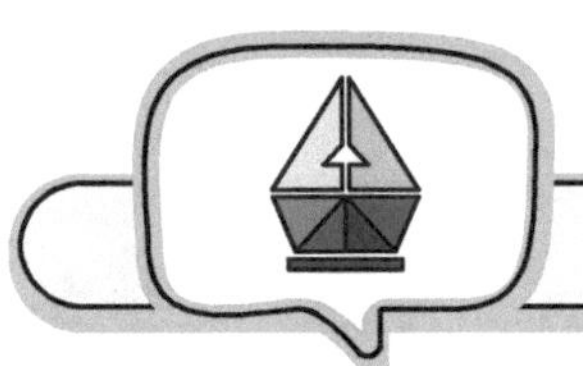

Week 5 • Activity 2

Transition Word Scavenger Hunt

Directions: Read the following sentences and underline all of the transitional words you find. An example has been done for you.

Example:
Choosing a new puppy is an exciting adventure. <u>First</u>, you need to consider how much time you can dedicate to playing with your new dog. <u>Next</u>, consider if you have an active or laid-back lifestyle. <u>Additionally</u>, you may want to spend some time with different breeds to get a sense of their personalities.

1. Walking in a forest can be a very relaxing activity. However, there are some precautions you need to take. During the winter, be sure to wear extra layers of clothing. Also, take a snack in case you stay out longer than you had planned.

2. Visiting the zoo allows you to observe animals up close. Additionally, there are often educational facts listed about the animals near their habitats. You may find that you really enjoy being around the animals. As a result, you might even decide to volunteer to help out!

3. While some people enjoy playing sports, others enjoy acting. If you would like to act, here are some things to keep in mind. First, watch lots of plays. You can learn so much just by watching other actors. Second, don't be afraid to mess up. All actors flub their lines from time to time; however, you can't let mistakes stop you from being on the stage.

4. Since my friend moved to Texas, we spend a lot more time texting. Despite the challenges of distance, technology has helped us remain close. Consequently, I still consider her my best friend.

5. Johnathan baked the cookies while I decorated the cake. We were running late to the bake sale, therefore, we didn't have a moment to lose. We ended up making it just in time because Ms. Paxton gave us a ride.

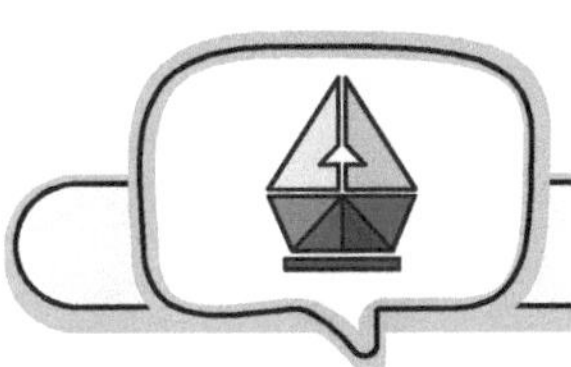

Week 5 • Activity 3

Telling the Difference

Directions: Read the words or phrases below and determine if they are concrete or abstract. Circle the correct answer. An example has been done for you.

Friendship

Concrete or (Abstract)

1. Chocolate Ice Cream

Concrete or Abstract

2. Honesty

Concrete or Abstract

3. Courage

Concrete or Abstract

4. Homework

Concrete or Abstract

5. Dreams

Concrete or Abstract

6. Basketball

Concrete or Abstract

7. Hope

Concrete or Abstract

8. Rain

Concrete or Abstract

9. Turtles

Concrete or Abstract

10. Laughter

Concrete or Abstract

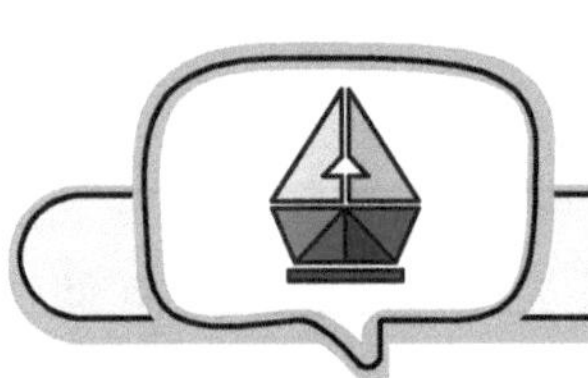

Week 5 • Activity 4

Removing the Concrete

Directions: Read the following sentences and then rewrite them to be vague. Pay attention to taking out concrete and descriptive words. An example has been done for you.

Example:

I go to Starbucks on Fridays and order a tall latte with a shot of caramel.

Make it vague: I go to the coffee shop every week and order a drink with an extra shot of flavor.

1. My Siamese cat turned ten years old on Wednesday.

....

....

....

2. The frozen lake gleamed in the bright afternoon sunshine.

....

....

....

3. The smell of scotch tape reminds me of wrapping Christmas presents on my grandmother's kitchen table.

....

....

....

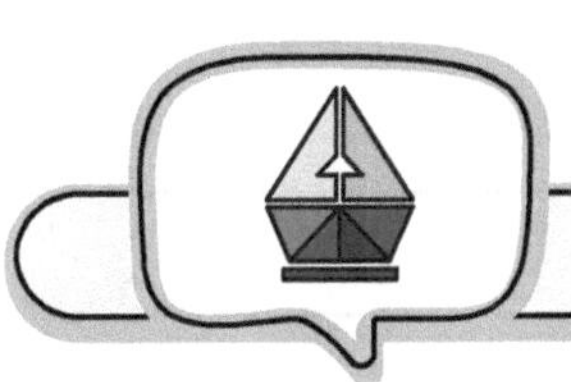

Week 5 • Activity 4

4. If you go five miles past the QT gas station, you will see our blue Victorian house on the left.

5. I was swimming in my aunt's pool and the chlorine smell brought back memories of the five summers I spent at Camp Womback as a child.

6. I got my father a plaid flannel shirt for his thirty-ninth birthday.

7. The temperature was twenty-nine degrees last night at midnight, but the wind chill made it feel like it was ten degrees.

8. The taste of a ripe watermelon always takes me back to that summer night in 2019 when I met Josh at the county fair.

9. In the winter, the needles from the pine trees that run along the east side of our property cover the ground like an old brown quilt.

10. Tomorrow we will write a five page essay for our History class about the Civil War.

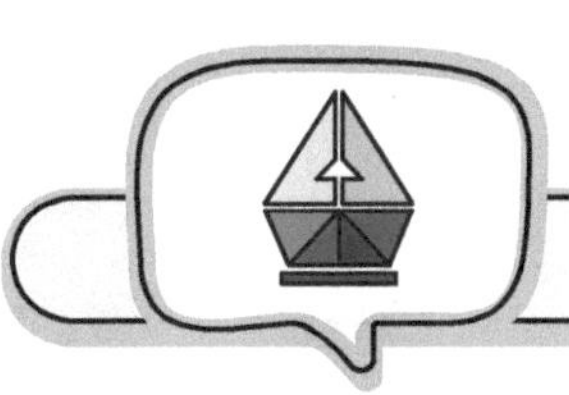

Week 5 • Activity 5

Add a Little Concrete

Directions: Change the following vague sentences to more precise sentences by adding concrete words. Remember to be specific and focus on the five senses. An example has been done for you.

Example:

Vague: My mother needs a new dress soon.

Concrete: My mother needs a new formal dress for my cousin's wedding in July.

1. The cat cleaned its fur.

2. She danced to a song for the talent show.

3. We had a lot of snow yesterday, so today we played.

4. We went out to eat.

5. I like this pie!

6. You make me happy.

7. The bird flew south for the winter.

8. His car suits his personality.

9. Sometimes we go to that store to buy clothes.

10. Nell likes to listen to music when she does her homework.

WEEK 6

Choosing Punctuation

This week, you'll learn about another important part of writing: choosing punctuation. Punctuating your sentences correctly helps a reader understand what you mean and how to read the sentence.

Choosing Punctuation

This week you are going to learn about **punctuation.** Understanding **punctuation** is important to writing correctly. Like word choice, punctuation helps the reader understand the sentence's emotions, meanings, and context.

Punctuation divides sentences into various parts and helps make them easy to read and understand. Without **punctuation** marks, it would be impossible to know where sentences begin or end. It would also be very difficult to know the meaning of the sentence. Let's look at an example:

Toss me the ball

Toss me the ball!

Without any **punctuation** in the first sentence, the reader does not know what is the mood of the sentence. In the next sentence, an exclamation point is used so the reader understands that the speaker is excited to have the ball tossed to them.

Now let's looks at types of **punctuation** you need to know in order to write effectively.

1. Full Stop. The full stop is the major punctuation that ends a sentence. Full stop punctuation marks consist of periods **(.)**, exclamation points **(!)** and question marks **(?)**. They help readers to understand where one sentence ends and another begins. Though the punctuation marks used may differ, every sentence ends with a full stop.

2. Comma **(,)**. A comma helps to divide the sentence or separate a list within a sentence. Look at the following two examples. In the first example, the comma is used to divide the sentence when it contains two thoughts that otherwise should be separated by a full stop. In the second example, the commas are used to separate a list.

Example: I love to play football, but my brother prefers soccer.

Example: I need you to pick up bananas, milk, paper towels, and soup at the grocery store.

Before we move on, let's learn about the Oxford Comma. The Oxford Comma comes at the end of the second to last item in the list. So in this list, the highlighted comma is the Oxford comma: "lemons, oranges**,** and grapes." You can also write this list as "lemons, oranges and grapes." Both ways are correct; the most important thing is to be consistent with either using the Oxford Comma or not.

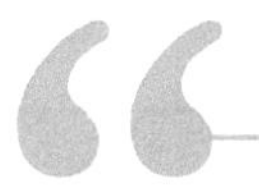

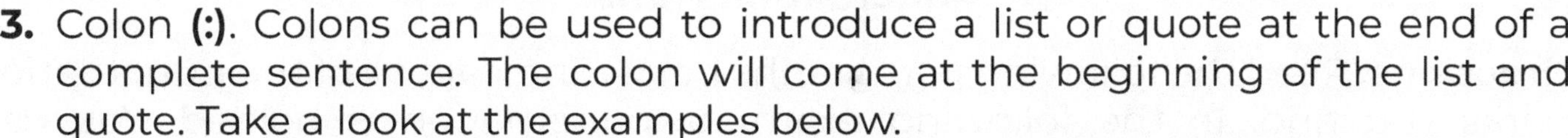

3. Colon (**:**). Colons can be used to introduce a list or quote at the end of a complete sentence. The colon will come at the beginning of the list and quote. Take a look at the examples below.

   Example: These are some of my favorite colors: purple, pink, green, brown.

   Example: Shakespeare said it best: "Though she be but little, she is fierce."

4. You learned in week three to use a comma when quoting someone in dialogue, so how do you know when to use a comma and when to use a colon? You use a colon when the quote comes after an **independent clause**. An independent clause can stand on its own as a sentence.

Example: Shakespeare said, "Though she be but little, she is fierce." The words introducing the quote, "Shakespeare said" cannot stand on their own as a complete sentence.

However, as in the example above, "Shakespeare said it best," can stand on its own as a complete sentence.

5. Semicolon (**;**). Semicolons can be used when you want to connect two independent clauses that could stand alone as a sentence. The second sentence will always depend on the first sentence for context. Here's an example.

   Example: Let's go to the library; there are five books I want to check out.

6. Apostrophe (**'**). An apostrophe is used to either to combing two words by omitting letters or to show ownership.

Example: I've got a lot of homework to do tonight. [The word "I've" in the sentence combines the words 'I' and 'have.']

Example: Brett's kitten is two months old. [In this sentence, the apostrophe in "Brett's" indicates that the kitten belongs to Brett.]

7. Hyphen (**-**). A hyphen is used to combine words. When you read the word, you can understand the meaning of the sentence more accurately. A hyphen is also used when spelling numbers. A hyphen should always be used when writing numbers between 21 and 99. The hyphen shows that the two numbers belong to each other. Here are two examples:

   Example: We booked a round-trip flight to Mexico.

   Example: My grandfather turned eighty-five on Monday.

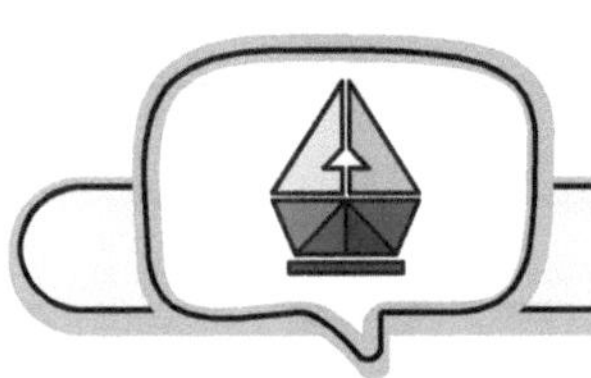

Week 6 • Activity 1

Punctuation Hunt

Directions: Read the following paragraphs below. Indicate all of the punctuation marks you find. In the following example, punctuation is bolded. You can underline or circle the punctuation in your hunt. An example has been done for you.

Example: I hope you**'**ll come to my party**.** We**'**ll have all of my favorite things **:** games **,** pinatas **,** cakes **,** bounce houses **,** ice creams**.**

In the heart of a bustling city, a little girl named Lily clutched her favorite stuffed bear, Button. With a tuft of worn-out fur and a missing eye, Button was more than just a toy; he was Lily's steadfast friend. One fateful day, Lily and her family decided to go to a lively carnival. Lily held Button tight and whispered to him about all of the fun things they were about to do.

Amidst the twinkling lights and merry-go-round music, a whirlwind of excitement enveloped Lily. Her laughter echoed through the air as she spun around on the carousel. Unbeknownst to her, in the midst of the joyous chaos, Button slipped from her grasp, tumbling into the crowd like a silent adventurer. Panic set in when Lily realized her cherished companion was missing. Frantically searching through the sea of carnival-goers, Lily's eyes welled with tears, and her heart sank with each passing moment.

Meanwhile, Button embarked on an unexpected journey of his own. From one set of curious hands to another, he became a silent witness to the carnival's magic. As the night unfolded, a kind soul noticed the lost bear and placed him on a vendor's booth. There, under the warm glow of carnival lights, Button patiently waited for Lily.

As the night wore on and Lily's search grew more desperate, her parents consoled her with the promise of a surprise that would make her forget the loss of Button: a bag of pink cotton candy, her favorite carnival treat. Lily, however, was too upset to even care. She walked glumly beside her parents up to the cotton candy vendor. As her parents ordered, Lily looked up to wipe the tears from her eyes with the sleeve of her shirt. To her surprise, there sat Button. The vendor gently placed him back in her arms. "I'll never let you go again!" Lily exclaimed.

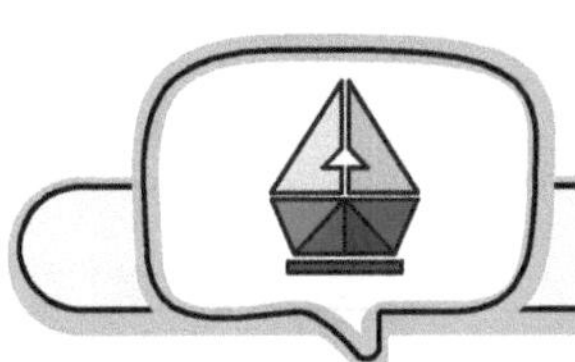

Week 6 • Activity 2

Fill in the Blanks

Directions: In the following activity, fill in the blanks in each sentence with the correct punctuation mark. An example has been done for you.

Example: ....“.... Where are you going ....?.... ....”.... Jane asked ....•....

1. If we....re going to decorate .... we need to go all out ....

2. She turned twenty....two in March ..... .

3. Albert Einstein said it best........Learn from yesterday.... live for today.... hope for tomorrow ....

4. Bring the water bucket over here.... I can....t wash the car without it....

5. My favorite school subjects.... History.... English.... Art.... Spanish....

6. Do you know when Hanukkah starts this year....

7. My brother....s mother....in....law is sick....

8. We....ve got a plan to make this Hunter....s best year yet....

9. Tomorrow....s forecast calls for snow.... so school will be canceled....

10. ....You shouldn....t be here........ Emily whispered....

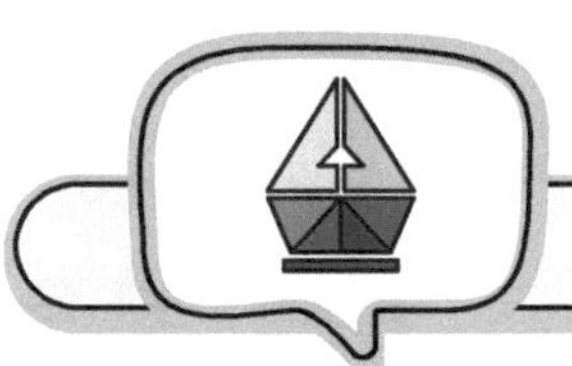

Week 6 • Activity 3

Full Stops

Directions: The following paragraph is full of run-on sentences. Read through it, and insert an appropriate full stop punctuation mark where needed. Be sure to capitalize the first word in the next sentence.

Example: We need to run to the store we're out of milk

We need to run to the store. We're out of milk.

In the early morning sunlight, armed with shovels, seeds, and the determination to create a vibrant garden that would be the envy of the neighborhood, I ventured into the backyard it was a patch of land that had long been neglected, overrun with weeds and devoid of any signs of life it sat waiting to be transformed into colorful blooms and delicious vegetables undeterred by the challenge that lay ahead, I started by turning over the soil breaking through the earth with the shovel was hard work soon I was digging into the garden with my hands to cover the seeds with the freshly turned soil as the sun climbed higher in the sky, casting its warm rays upon me, I began to sweat I knew my efforts would be rewarded a few weeks later when the sprouts would push through the earth have you ever planted a garden

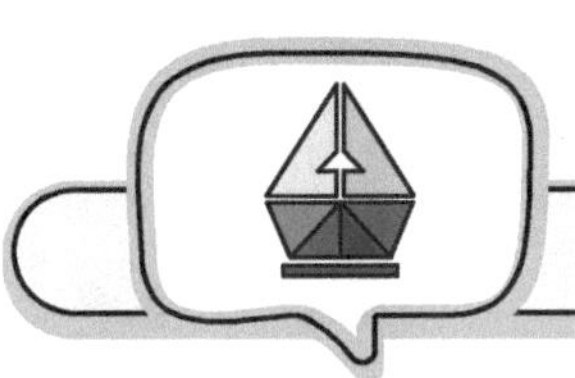

Week 6 • Activity 4

Time for a Pause

Directions: Read the following sentences and insert commas where necessary. An example has been done for you.

Example: : In the morning we will get up eat breakfast and go to school.

In the morning**,** we will get up**,** eat breakfast**,** and go to school.

1. "First you will want to get out a piece of paper" our teacher said.
2. My teacher thinks I am bright funny and respectful.
3. Under the oak tree we buried a necklace a map and a diary.
4. Since you like to draw will you illustrate the cartoon for me?
5. My best friend Sarah loves to read adventure books.
6. We went to the park played on the swings and had a picnic.
7. In the morning I have cereal and in the evening I eat dinner with my family.
8. The dog a playful Labrador chased the ball across the yard.
9. Lisa said "Here it's the book I promised you."
10. I got a few things for my birthday: a new coat a brown pocketbook a ticket to the ballgame a gift card to my favorite store.

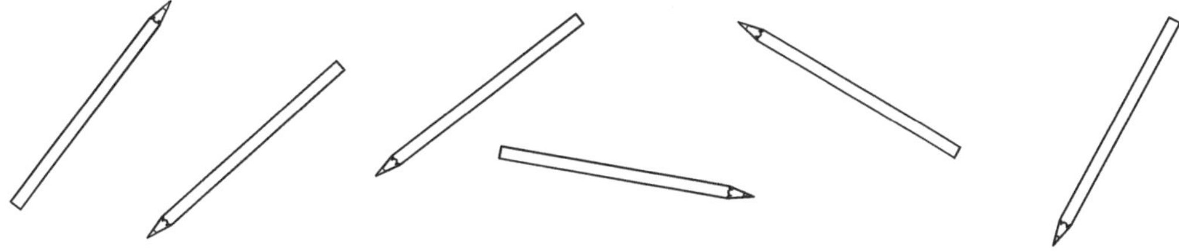

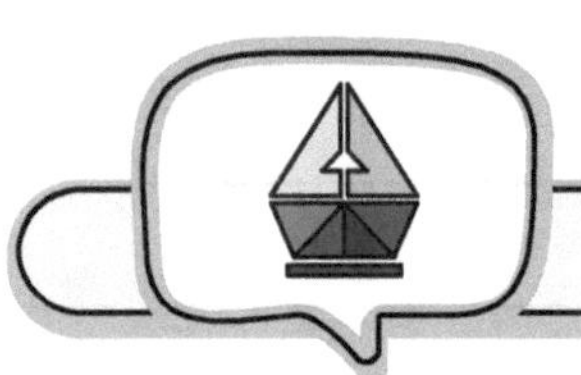

Week 6 • Activity 5

Semicolon/Colon True or False

Directions: Indicate whether the following statements are true or false. Mark **T** for true or **F** for false before each statement. An example has been done for you.

Example: ...T... Semicolons and colons are the same thing.

1. .... A semicolon is used to join two independent clauses.

2. .... A semicolon can be used to introduce a list.

3. .... A semicolon can be used before a quote if the words introducing the quote cannot stand on their own.

4. .... The weather is cold; however, we still decided to go for a walk. -that sentence is written correctly.

5. .... When using colons, the second sentence will always be dependent on the first.

6. .... A colon can be used to introduce a list.

7. .... A colon can be used before a quote if the words introducing the quote can stand on their own.

8. .... If you go down the road; you will find a creek. -that sentence is written correctly.

9. .... Colons and semicolons look the same.

10. .... My mother always reminds me: "Make your bed before you leave in the morning." -that sentence is written correctly.

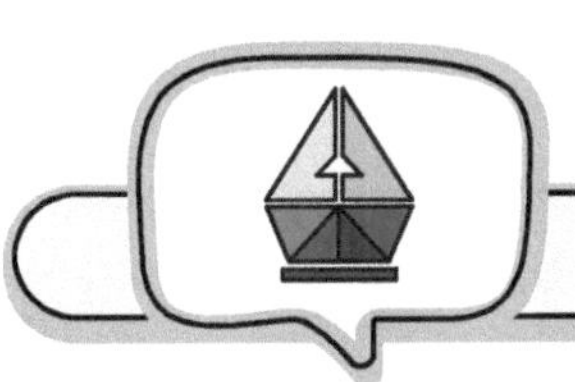

Week 6 • Activity 6

Q & A

Directions: Answer the following questions about punctuation. An example has been done for you.

Example: Question: Can an apostrophe be used to combine two words?

Answer: Yes

1. Question: What are two reasons punctuation is important?
   Answer:

2. Question: What are three punctuation marks that will end a sentence full stop?
   Answer:

3. Question: What are two reasons apostrophes are used?
   Answer:

4. Question: What numbers do you always hyphenate when spelling?
   Answer:

5. Question: What is required in order to use a colon before a quote?
Answer:

6. Question: Semicolons are used to connect what?
Answer:

7. Question: What are two reasons to use a comma?
Answer:

8. Question: What punctuation does every sentence contain?
Answer:

9. Question: What is an Oxford Comma?
Answer:

10. Question: If you want to use a colon to make a list, what needs to come before it?
Answer:

WEEK 7

Narrative Writing: Conclusions

This week we will wrap up on our learning about narrative writing by learning to close out our writing pieces in the best way.

This week you're going to learn about **conclusions** in narrative writing. Think of the **conclusion** like writing on a cake; just like "Happy Birthday Mom" written on a cake lets everyone know the reason the cake was baked and that its purpose is to celebrate Mom's birthday, the **conclusion** lets your reader know why you wrote the narrative and what you hope your writing has accomplished.

With the **conclusion**, you want to tie up any loose ends and answer any remaining questions the reader might have. **Conclusions** should leave the reader with a sense of satisfaction and completion.

Sometimes writing **conclusions** can feel like the most difficult part of writing your narrative. We're going to look at six ways to conclude your narrative. Depending on your subject, you may want to focus on one or more of these items in your conclusion.

1. **Summarize the main points.** This is a particularly good option if you are writing an essay in which you are trying to explain something complex or argue for or against a point.

   Example: In conclusion, going to bed every night at the same time can help you feel more rested and accomplish more throughout the day.

2. **Add something personal.** If writing something instructional or technical, here is your chance to insert your own personal thoughts and feelings about the subject.

   Example: Learning to sew may be difficult, but it has added a great deal of pleasure to my life. I find it helps me unwind after a difficult day and it has provided me with a skill I can use to give my friends and family meaningful gifts.

3. **End with a moral or lesson learned.** This can be an effective ending for personal stories and fictional stories. If the purpose of telling the story is to share something that you or a character learned, the conclusion of the narrative is the time to state it plainly so that the reader knows exactly what you hope they take away from your story.

   Example: The hare learned that the fastest one doesn't always cross the finish line first.

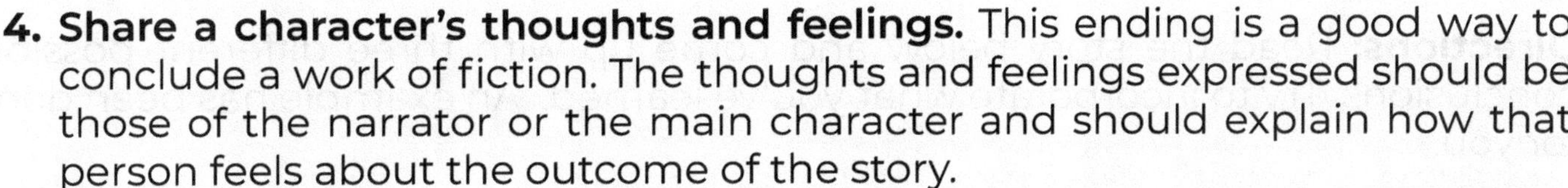

4. **Share a character's thoughts and feelings.** This ending is a good way to conclude a work of fiction. The thoughts and feelings expressed should be those of the narrator or the main character and should explain how that person feels about the outcome of the story.

   Example: Holden mourned the loss of his innocence. Although he still felt angry at the way things had ended, he knew he was strong enough to face the future.

5. **Explain the effect.** This conclusion works well for both fiction and non-fiction. Let's say you are writing a narrative about a war. The main part of your narrative may focus on the war itself, but a conclusion explaining the aftereffects of the war is a good way to provide the reader with additional information without needing to elaborate.

   Example: Although the Civil War ended, the road to freedom had just begun.

6. **End with hope for the future.** While it's not true that every story has a happy ending, it never hurts! This ending works especially well if your narrative has been sad or dealing with a difficult topic. Provide the reader with the knowledge that all is not lost, and better days are coming.

   Example: While the effects of climate change seem overwhelming, scientists are hard at work to create new ways to save the planet.

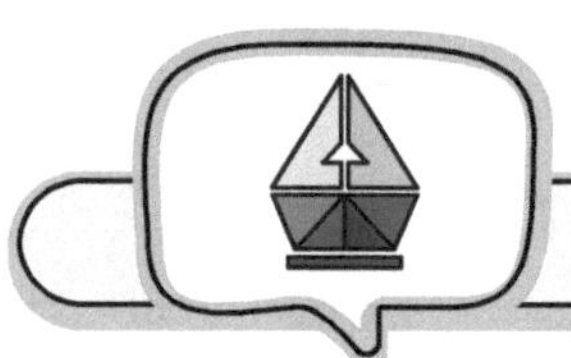

Spitball Endings

Directions: Read the story below and come up with three different possible conclusions. Try to incorporate what you've learned. An example has been done for you.

Example:

Story: Sam went to the amusement park with his friends. Although he had never been on a roller-coaster, his friends talked him into it. He got more and more nervous as they waited in the long line. Finally, it was Sam's turn to board. He shared a seat with his best friend, Jimmy. He tried to remain calm as the car slowly clicked its way to the top of the huge hill. He shut his eyes and held his breath, waiting for the drop.

Possible Ending: In the very next instant, Sam was flying downward and Jimmy squealed with delight beside him. He gripped the seat bar in front with all of his might and kept his eyes shut tight as he was jostled back and forth. "Open your eyes!" Jimmy yelled at him. Sam wanted to face his fears, so he made himself open his eyes, just in time to see the roller-coaster climbing another hill. This time he kept his eyes open and discovered he loved the thrill! Just like that, the ride was over, but this time it was Sam who talked his friends into going again.

Now it's your turn!

Story: As the plane touched down in the tropical paradise, excitement filled my body. Family vacations were a cherished tradition, and this trip was no exception. I was looking forward to swimming in the ocean, shopping with my mom, and all of the wonderful seafood dinners my dad would prepare for us. However, on the first evening, as the sun dipped below the horizon, I saw my parents exchange a worried glance. "Is everything ok?" I asked.

"Of course, dear," said my mother, but afterwards she looked nervously at my father. Later that night, I heard whispers coming from their room. The next morning, I awoke to find my parents gone, but a rather large package that I had never seen before was sitting on the kitchen table.

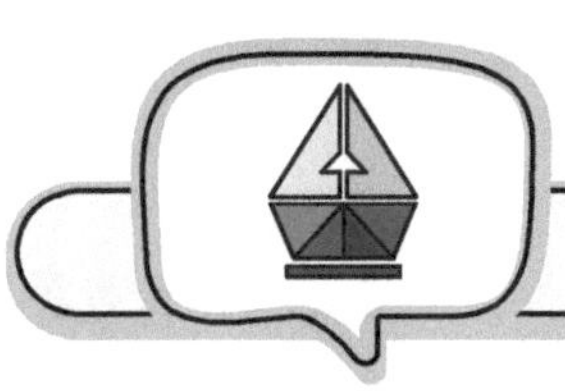

Possible Ending #1:

Possible Ending #2:

Possible Ending #3:

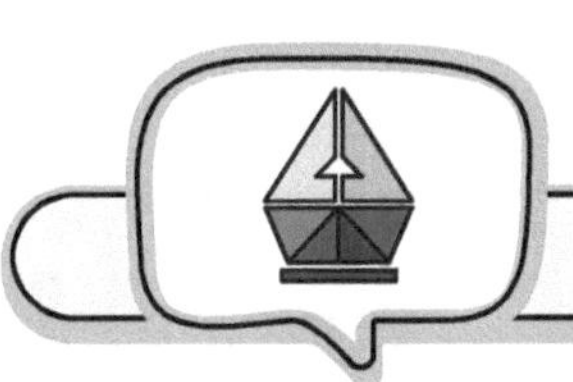

Week 7 • Activity 2

Make It Personal

Directions: Read the story ideas below. Create a personal story conclusion for each. An example has been done for you.

Example:

Story Idea: A boy visits an animal shelter for the first time.

Personal Conclusion: I will never forget that day at the shelter. The love I felt for the animals I met and the sadness that tugged at my heart imagining them without a home stayed with me long after I left the building. Looking back, I believe that was the first day I knew I would eventually become an animal advocate.

Now it's your turn!

Story Idea: #1: Grandma accidently uncovers a box of buried treasure while tending her roses.

Personal Conclusion:

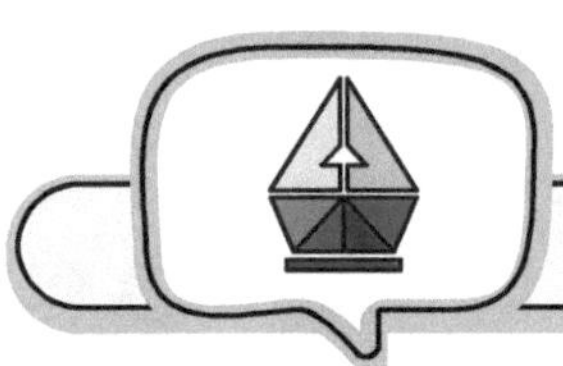

Week 7 • Activity 2

Story Idea: #2: Casey accidentally gets locked in the mall overnight.

Personal Conclusion:

Story Idea: #3: The time I learned the value of friendship.

Personal Conclusion:

WEEK 8

Greek and Latin Root Words

This week, we'll be taking a break from narrative writing, and we'll be learning about special parts of words. Greek and Latin roots are parts of words that affect their meeting.

Greek and Latin Root Words

This week you will learn about Greek and Latin **root words. Root words** are base words from which other words are formed. These are the core words that carry the main meaning of the word. Think of them as the building blocks of the English language.

You may be wondering, what is the difference between a Greek **root word** and a Latin **root word?** Greek and Latin are two different languages, just like English and Spanish are different languages.

Greek is about two thousand years older than Latin. However, Greek is what is called a "living" language, meaning there are people in the word that still speak it today. Latin is a "dead" language, meaning it is no longer used in everyday life.

For our purposes here, it isn't important to know which language the **root word** comes from.

On the following two pages, you will find charts of some of the most commonly used Greek and Latin **root words**. Study these charts and then use them to help you complete this week's activities.

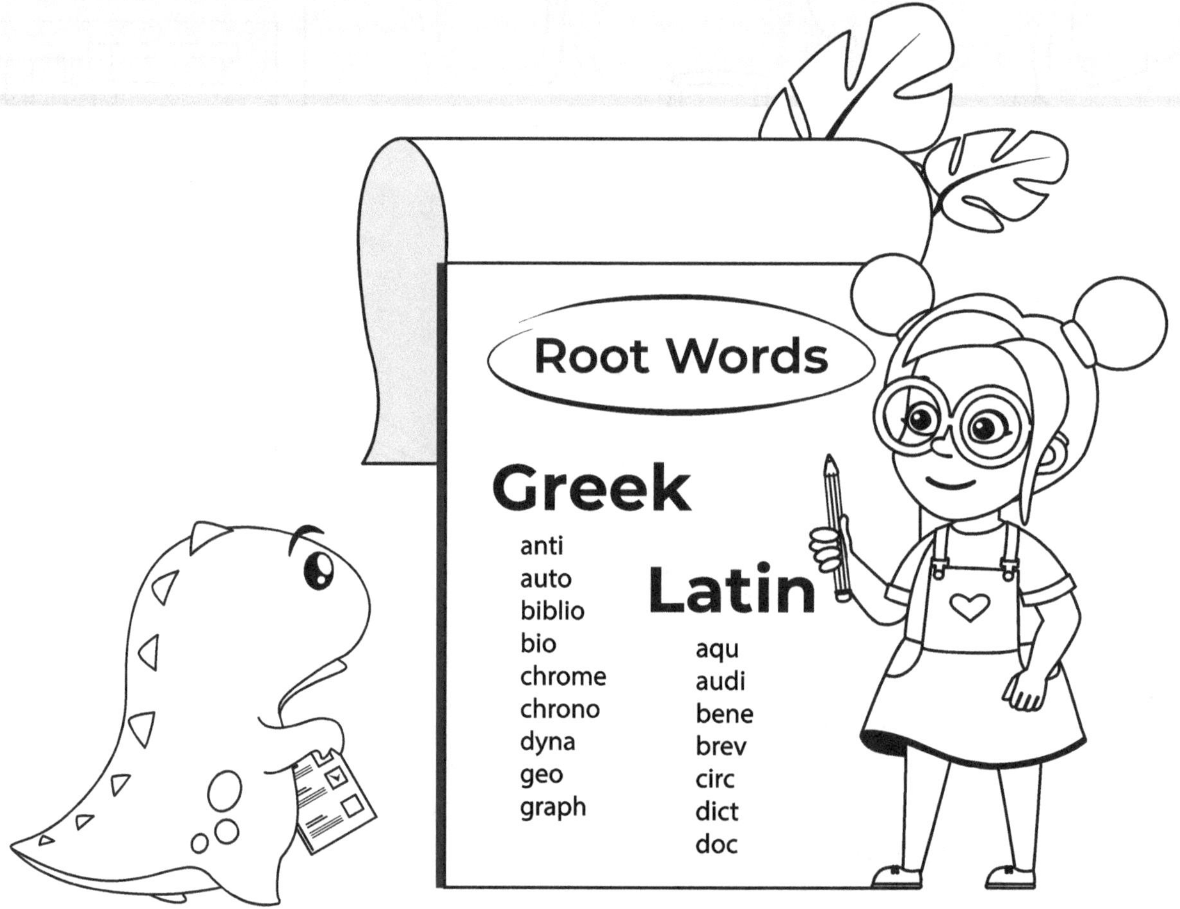

Greek and Latin Root Words

Common Greek Root Words		Common Latin Root Words	
Root	Meaning	Root	Meaning
anti	against	aqu	water
auto	self	audi	hear
biblio	book	bene	good
bio	life	brev	short
chrome	color	circ	round
chrono	time	dict	say
dyna	power	doc	teach
geo	earth	duc	lead, make
graph	write	gen	to birth
hydr	water	hab	to have
log	thought	lev	to lift
logos	word, study	luc, lum	light
pac	peace	manu	hand
path	feel	pac	peace
phil	love	port	carry
phon	sound	scrib, script	to write
photo	light	sens	to feel
schem	plan	terr	earth
syn	together, with	tim	to fear
tele	far	vid, vis	to see

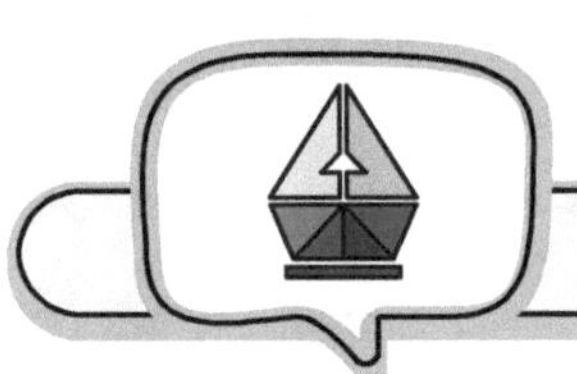

Week 8 • Activity 1

Match the Meaning

Directions: In the following activity, draw a line matching the root word to its meaning. An example has been done for you.

Example:

tim — time

chrono — to fear

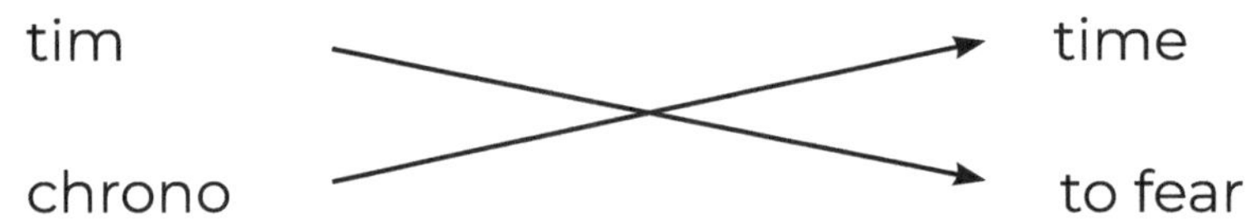

Root Word	Meaning
Geo	Together
Auto	Self
Doc	Lead
Scrib	Thought
Biblio	Good
Duc	Earth
Log	Book
Phon	Teach
Syn	Sound
Bene	Write

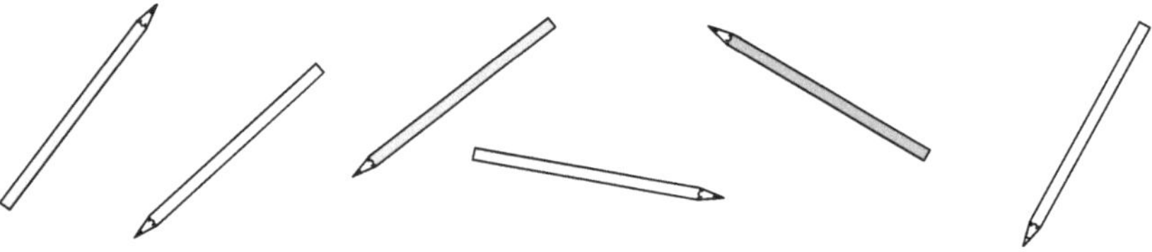

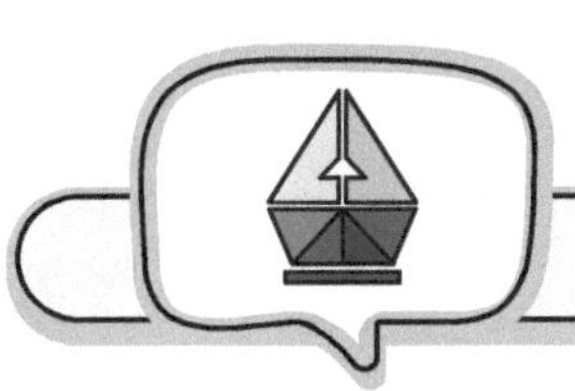

Week 8 • Activity 2

What Does It Mean?

Directions: In this activity, you will be given words that all contain the same root. See if you can figure out what the root word means. An example has been done for you.

Example:

Words: Audio, Audible, Auditorium Meaning: Hear

1. Words: Video, Vision Meaning: ....
2. Words: Dynamite, Dynamic Meaning: ....
3. Words: Telephone, Television Meaning: ....
4. Words: Circle, Circumvent Meaning: ....
5. Words: Phone, Phonetic Meaning: ....
6. Words: Benefit, Beneficial Meaning: ....
7. Words: Portable, Import Meaning: ....
8. Words: Hydrant, Hydrate Meaning: ....
9. Words: Generation, Genetic Meaning: ....
10. Words: Timid, Intimidate Meaning: ....

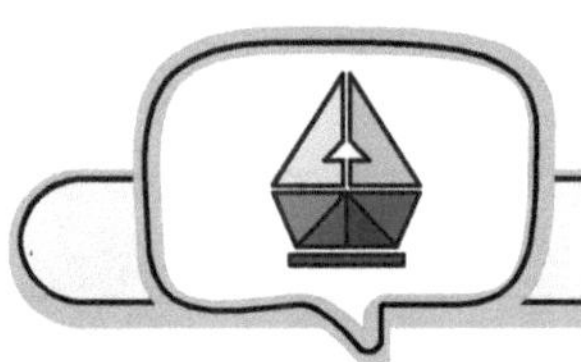

Week 8 • Activity 3

Find the Root

Directions: In this activity, you will be given a word and its dictionary definition. Underline the root word within the word given. An example has been done for you, with the root word highlighted.

Example: Terrain – a piece of land.

1. Illuminate – to brighten with light.

2. Geography – the study of the physical features of the earth.

3. Manuscript – a handwritten or typed piece of writing

4. Photography – the art, science, or practice of creating images by recording light on a sensitive surface.

5. Benevolent – characterized by goodwill or kindly feelings.

6. Invisible – unable to be seen.

7. Aquatic – living in or near the water.

8. Pacify – to bring peace or tranquility.

9. Brevity – shortness of duration.

10. Monochrome – made with a single color or hue.

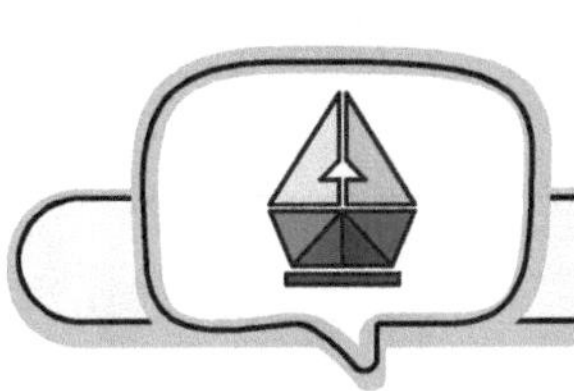

Week 8 • Activity 4

Directions: Write as many words as you know that contain the root word given. An example has been done for you.

Example: Root Word: lev – elevate, levitate, level, alleviate, levy

1. Root Word: tele

2. Root Word: graph

3. Root Word: anti

4. Root Word: auto

5. Root Word: hab

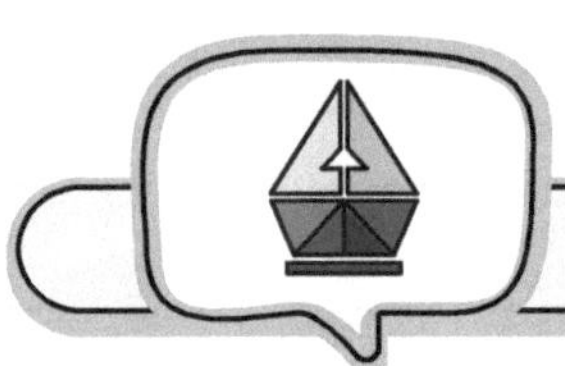

6. Root Word: dict

7. Root Word: port

8. Root Word: sens

9. Root Word: vis

10. Root Word: photo

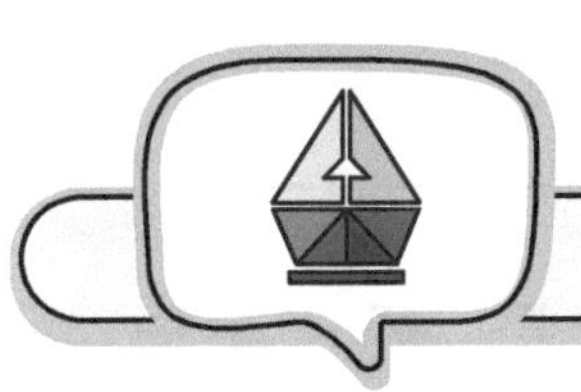

Week 8 • Activity 5

Root Word Hunt

Directions: The following sentences have at least one word that contains a root word that you have been studying. Some sentences have more than one word. Underline the words that contain a root word. An example has been done for you.

Example: During the science fair, the students came up with a clever scheme to showcase their inventions, and they used their creative manual skills to build impressive models and displays.

1. For the school talent show, the students collaborated on a creative dance routine, using a clever scheme to synchronize their moves and make the performance truly spectacular.
2. During our field trip to the aquarium, we were amazed by all of the colorful marine life swimming in the tanks.
3. My dad had to take his automobile into the mechanic because the check engine light was illuminated.
4. During the science fair, Emma decided to document her experiment with detailed notes.
5. At the school carnival, Jake showed his strong sense of philanthropy by organizing a "Pet Adoption" booth.
6. Meeting Taylor Swift in person was amazing! After taking a photograph with her, I asked for her autograph and she signed my t-shirt.
7. We learned all about the life cycle of butterflies in biology class.
8. The way the characters solved the mystery in the play was totally illogical, but it made us laugh.
9. In church, we pray before reading the Holy Scripture.
10. Yesterday, we learned about using apostrophes to abbreviate words.

WEEK 9

Affixes: Prefixes and Suffixes

Building on your knowledge from last week, we'll learn about a few other word parts that alter what a word means.

ARGOPREP

Affixes: Prefixes and Suffixes

This week we will build upon the root words you learned last week by learning about **affixes.** Remember that root words are base words that carry the meaning of the word.

Affixes are small groups of letters that are added to the beginning **(prefixes)** or the ending **(suffixes)** of a word to change its inflection or meaning.

Understanding **affixes** is important in order to convey precise meaning in your writing. Learning about **affixes** will help you with spelling and can help you figure out what new words mean.

Prefixes are **affixes** that come at the beginning of a word to either change its inflection or meaning. For example, a common **prefix** is un-. Un- means not. Adding the **prefix** un- to the word happy now changes its meaning to the opposite of happy. If you are unhappy, then you are not happy.

Likewise, **suffixes** are **affixes** that are added to the end of a word to change its form or meaning. A common **suffix** is –er. Adding the **suffix** –er to the word play changes the meaning of the word from a game to the one who plays the game, the player.

Sometimes, adding a **suffix** will change the spelling of the original word. This can be tricky, but here are six rules to help guide you in spelling words with **suffixes** correctly.

Rule 1: Double the Consonant.

Adding suffixes to some base words that end with a consonant will require you to double the last letter, but this only applies in certain situations.

When a word ends in a short vowel sound followed by a single consonant, the last letter of the word will be doubled before adding the suffix.

Example: **fat + er = fatter**

Example: **mud + y = muddy**

When a word has more than one syllable and ends in "L," you will need to double the "L" before adding the suffix.

Example: **cancel + ed = cancelled**

Example: **fulfil + ment = fulfillment**

This rule does not apply to words that end in "w," "x," or "y."

Rule 2: Drop the Silent E

When a word ends in a silent letter "e" and you are adding a suffix that begins with a vowel, then drop the final "e." If the suffix begins with a consonant, you do not drop the silent "e."

Example: **drive + -ing = driving**

Example: **make + er = maker**

Example of not dropping the silent "e": **settle + ment = settlement**

Rule 3: Keep the Final E

There are four times that you will keep the final "e."

1. Words ending in –ee, -oe, or –ye: the silent "e" is usually retained to maintain the pronunciation of the root word.

   Example: **agree + able = agreeable**

   Example: **canoe + ing = canoe**

   Example: **dye + ing = dyeing**

2. Words with a soft "c" or "g" before the silent "e": if the word ends in a soft "c" or "g," the silent "e" is kept to maintain the pronunciation.

   Example: **peace + able = peaceable**

3. When you add the suffix –ly or –ful: you always keep the silent "e" when adding –ly and -ful

   Example: **love + ly = lovely**

   Example: **care + ful = careful**

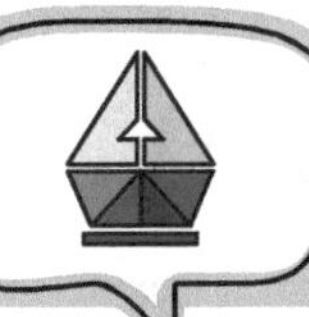

Affixes: Prefixes and Suffixes

Rule 4: Keep the Final Y

There are two instances when you will keep the final "y" when adding a suffix.

1. If the word ends in "y" and has a vowel before the "y," then keep the "y" when adding the suffix.

   Example: **enjoy + ed = enjoyed**

2. If the word ends in "y" and the suffix starts with an "i." A word cannot have two i's in a row.

   Example: **copy + ing = copying.**

Rule 5: Change the Y to and I

When a word has a consonant before the "y," change the "y" to "i" before adding the suffix.

Example: **beauty + ful = beautiful**

There will be some exceptions to this rule that don't follow any reasoning. The best way to learn these is through reading where you will see them repeatedly.

Exception example: **baby + ish = babyish**

Rule 6: Change IE to Y

When a word ends in "ie," change the ending to a "y" before adding the suffix.

Example: **tie + ing = tying**

Study the charts of **prefixes** and **affixes** on the following two pages and then use them to help you complete this week's activities.

Affixes: Prefixes and Suffixes

Prefix	Meaning
un-	not
re-	again
pre-	before
post-	after
dis-	not, opposite
mis-	wrong
multi-	many, much
bi-	two
non-	not
in- (or il-, im-, ir-)	not
ex-	out of, former
sub-	under
inter-	between, among
over-	too much, above
under-	too little, below
semi-	half
micro-	small, tiny
macro-	large, long
co-	together, with
super-	above, beyond

Suffix	Meaning
-able	capable of
-ful	full of
-less	without
-er	one who
-est	most
-ly	like, in the manner of
-ment	action or process
-ness	state or quality
-ist	one who practices
-ity	state or quality
-ify	to make, to cause to be
-ive	having the nature of
-ous	full of, characterized by
-tion	action or process
-sion	state or quality
-ate	to make, to act
-ize	to make, to become
-al	relating to, like
-ic	pertaining to
-ship	position held, status

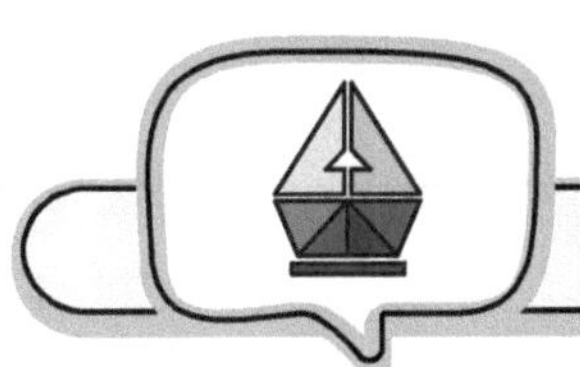

Week 9 • Activity 1

Match the Prefix

Directions: For this activity, draw a line to match the prefix with its meaning. An example has been done for you.

Example:

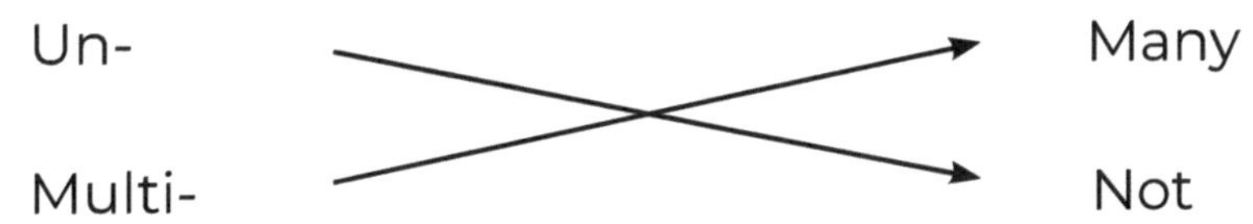

Prefix	Meaning
Sub-	Under
Inter-	Wrong
Semi-	After
Re-	Again
Post-	Between
Mis-	Small
Co-	Half
Micro-	Not
Macro-	Together
Dis-	Large

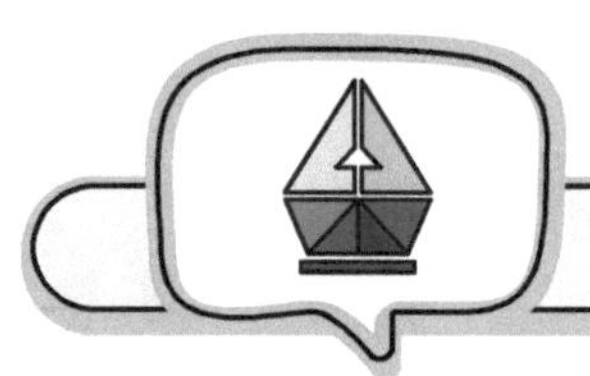

Prefix Generator

Directions: The following table provides you with a prefix, its meaning, and an example word that uses that prefix. For this activity, you write in the final column on the table at least two or more words that share the same prefix as the example word. An example has been done for you.

Example:

Prefix	Meaning	Example	Words that Share the Prefix
Multi	Many	Multipurpose	Multiple, Multinational

Prefix	Meaning	Example	Words that Share the Prefix
Re-	Again	Return	
Pre-	Before	Prehistoric	
Ex-	Out of, Former	Extra	
In-	Not	Inaccurate	
Bi-	Two	Bilateral	
Post-	After	Postpone	
Sub-	Under	Submarine	
Super-	Above, Beyond	Superlative	
Un-	Not	Uninterested	
Dis-	Not, Opposite	Disrupt	

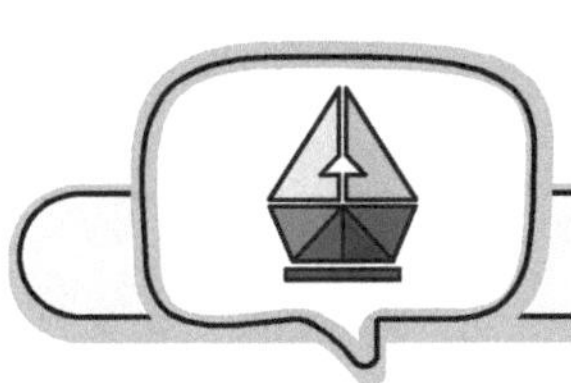

Match the Suffix

Directions: For this activity, draw a line to match the suffix with its meaning. An example has been done for you.

Example:

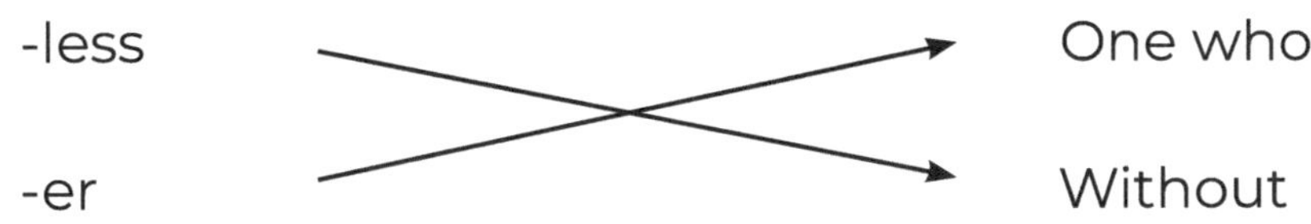

Suffix	Meaning
-ic	Action
-ify	Capable of
-ment	Full of
-ive	One who practices
-ous	Pertaining to
-able	State or quality
-ship	Position held
-al	To make
-ity	Having the nature of
-ist	Relating to

Spell It Out

Directions: In this activity, you will use the rules you learned about changing the spelling of a word when you add a suffix. Take the word and suffix given and combine them to spell the new word correctly. Pay attention to the rules you learned about when to change a word when adding a suffix. An example has been done for you.

Example: Change + able = Changeable

1. Definite + ly = ...

2. Joy + ful = ...

3. Courage + ous = ...

4. Control + ed = ...

5. Agree + ing = ...

6. Flavor + ful = ...

7. Trace + able = ...

8. True + est = ...

9. Lie + ing = ...

10. Try + ing = ...

Build a Word

Directions: In this activity you will add a prefix or a suffix of your choosing to the word listed to create a new word. Then write a sentence using your new word. An example has been done for you.

Example:

Word: Rule

Suffix: ......er......

Sentence: King Charles III became the ruler of England when Queen Elizabeth II passed away.

1. Word: Friend
   Suffix: ....
   Sentence:

....

....

....

2. Word: Use
   Prefix: ....
   Sentence:

....

....

....

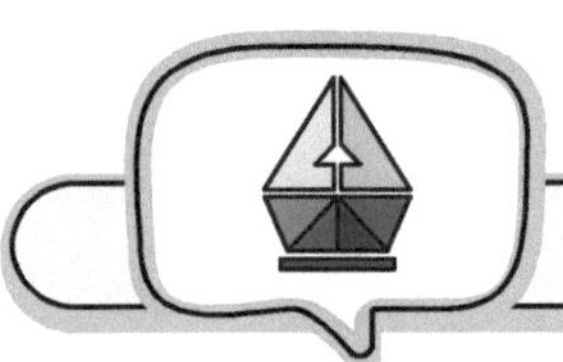

3. Word: Scope
Prefix: ....
Sentence:

....

....

....

4. Word: Person
Suffix: ....
Sentence:

....

....

....

5. Word: Hope
Suffix: ....
Sentence:

....

....

....

6. Word: Natural
Prefix: ....
Sentence:

....

....

....

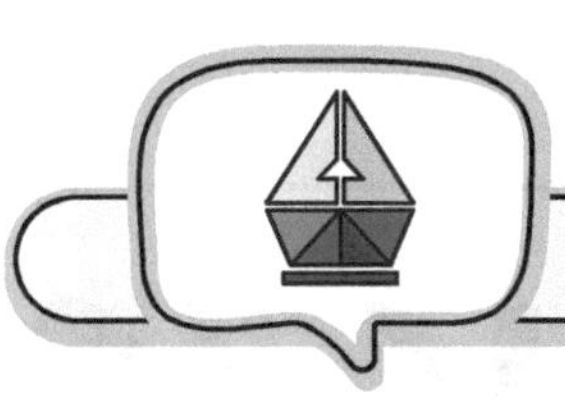

7. Word: Take

Prefix: ....

Sentence:

....

....

....

8. Word: Clean

Suffix: ....

Sentence:

....

....

....

9. Word: Real

Suffix: ....

Sentence:

....

....

....

10. Word: National

Prefix: ....

Sentence:

....

....

....

WEEK 10

This week you'll take a quick look at everything you've learned so far. Way to go!

Congratulations! You have finished half of this workbook. You have worked hard and learned so much over the last nine weeks. You should be very proud of yourself.

Now it's time for us to review what you've learned. As you read through this review and do the activities, pay special attention to the lessons that might have been a little bit harder for you. We covered lot of material; it's OK to need to repeat some of the lessons.

In week one, you learned about **similes** and **metaphors**. Both compare two things which may not seem to have much in common at first glance. The difference between the two is **similes** use the words "like" or "as," while **metaphors** say that one thing is the other.

For example, we can compare an Olympic athlete and the wind. Typically, humans and forces of nature don't share similar traits. However, we can compare an Olympic athlete to the wind to indicate that he or she moves as fast as the wind does. To make this comparison as a **simile**, we would write, "The Olympian runs like the wind." To make this comparison as a **metaphor**, we would write, "The Olympian is the wind."

Over the next two weeks, you learned about narrative writing. Specifically, you learned about **narrators** and **characters**, and **dialogue** and **descriptions**. Narrative writing tells a story and the **narrator** is the one who is telling it. The **narrator** can also be a **character** in the story; if this is the case, then it is called a first-person narrative. The story is told through the perspective of the **narrator** as they experienced it.

Sometimes, a writer will choose to write in third-person. If this is the case, the **narrator** is not a **character** in the story, but rather has an omniscient point-of-view. They know everything that is happening and know all of the characters' thoughts and feelings.

A narrative can also be written in second-person. In this type of narrative, the **narrator** speaks directly to the reader, making them feel like the main character. This workbook is written in second-person!

Review Week

In addition to the narrator who tells the story, every narrative contains **characters**. **Characters** are the people, animals, or things in the story that think, feel, or act. You learned about four major **character** types: the protagonist (the main character), the antagonist (the villain), the sidekick (someone who helps the main character), and minor characters (all other characters that do not play a major role in the narrative).

Characters come alive for the reader through **dialogue** and **description. Dialogue** is the exact words a **character** says. **Dialogue** needs to be properly punctuated in order to be understood. If you need to, take a moment to go back to Week 3 and review how to write **dialogue**.

Description brings the rest of the story to life for the reader. When writing **description**, focus on trying to make sure the reader experiences the narrative with all five of their senses.

You then learned about how to write good **description** by focusing on **word choice**, including **emotion words**, **transitional words**, and **concrete words. Word choice** helps the reader fully comprehend the characters and story.

Word choice conveys meaning. There are two types of usages — denotative and connotative. Denotative usage is a word's basic, dictionary definition and usage. Connotative usage is how the word is being used in a given context.

Transitional words help to tie ideas together and improve the flow of your writing. **Transitional words** may be a single word or word phrase, like "in conclusion." **Transitional words** can generally be grouped into five categories: time, location, addition, comparison and contrast, and cause and effect.

Concrete words describe real things, things that are tangible and can be experienced with the five senses. **Concrete words** keep writing from being vague and abstract by creating vivid pictures in the reader's mind.

Choosing the right **punctuation** can be just as important as choosing the right words. **Punctuation** divides sentences into various parts and helps make them easy to read and understand. You learned about six different kinds of **punctuation**: full stops **(. or ! or ?)**, commas **(,)**, colons **(:)**, semicolons **(;)**, apostrophes **(')**, hyphens **(-)**. If you need to take a moment to review how each of these punctuation marks are used, do so now.

Week 10  Review Week

The last thing you learned about narrative writing was the importance of having a strong **conclusion**. After reading the **conclusion**, the audience should have a clear understanding of why the narrative was written and should feel a sense of satisfaction and completion. There are many different ways to conclude a narrative: summarize the main points, end with a moral, add something personal, share the main character's thoughts and feelings, explain the effect, end with hope for the future.

Finally, you learned about **Greek and Latin root words** and **affixes. Root words** are the building blocks of the English language. They carry the main meaning of the word. **Affixes** are small groups of letters that are added to the beginning or the ending of words to change the words' inflections or meanings. **Prefixes**, which go at the beginning of the word, and **suffixes**, which go at the end of the word, are the two types of **affixes**.

Suffixes sometimes require you to change the way a word is spelled. It can be tricky knowing when and how to make those changes, but you learned five rules to make it easier. If you need to, go back and review those rules now.

Whew! You've really learned a lot. Let's do some activities to further review and practice all that you've learned.

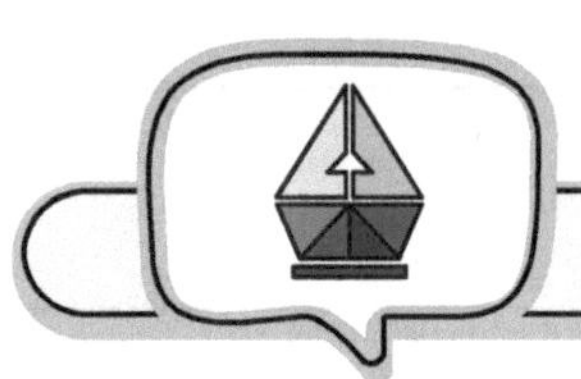

Week 10 • Activity 1

Similes and Metaphors – Knowing the Difference

Directions: In this activity, read the sentence and determine if the comparison is a simile or a metaphor. Write your answer in the space to the left. An example has been done for you.

Example: Metaphor – My love for you is a red rose.

1. .... My grandmother's quilt makes me feel as snug as a bug in a rug.

2. .... Her explanation was clear as a crystal, so we didn't need to ask questions.

3. .... Your laughter is music to my ears.

4. .... Carrying the pail of water felt light as a feather after picking up bricks all day.

5. .... The fog hung over the town like a soft, gray blanket.

6. .... The streets were rivers of cars after the football game let out.

7. .... The classroom was a beehive of activity before Winter Break.

8. .... The artist's hands were steady as a rock as he finished his masterpiece.

9. .... The internet is a vast ocean of information, waiting to be explored.

10. .... The forest is a cathedral of nature, still and filled with many wonders.

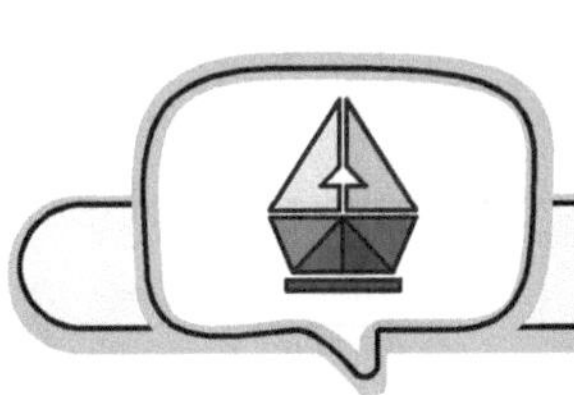

Week 10 • Activity 2

Fill in the Blank

Directions: In this activity, fill in the blanks with the correct word or words. An example has been done for you.

Example: ......Minor...... characters may never encounter the protagonist in a narrative.

1. .... – person narrators use the pronouns *I* and *we*.

2. The .... has a close relationship with the main character.

3. Second-person narrators speak directly to the ....

4. Dialogue is set apart from the rest of the narrative writing with .... marks.

5. A good way to add description to your narrative is by including the .... of a character.

6. When one character stops speaking and another one starts, this is indicated by a .... break.

7. The antagonist is the .... of the story.

8. A .... indicates who is speaking.

9. Second-person narrators use the pronouns .... and ....

10. When writing dialogue, question marks and exclamation points always go on the .... of the quotation marks.

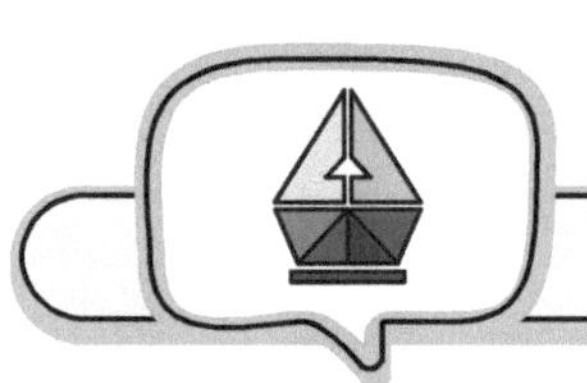

Week 10 • Activity 3

True or False

Directions: In this activity, indicate whether the statement is true or false by putting a **T** for true or an **F** for false in the space to the left of the statement. An example has been done for you.

Example: ......T...... The best way to build your vocabulary is to read.

1. .... When choosing a synonym, it's important to make sure you understand what makes the words slightly different from one another.
2. .... Word choice is one of the things that cannot create specificity.
3. .... Denotative describes a word's basic, dictionary definition and usage.
4. .... It isn't necessary to consider the audience when choosing words.
5. .... Connotative usage creates vague language.
6. .... Transitional words can generally be grouped into five categories.
7. .... Synonyms are words that mean the same thing.
8. .... "Furthermore" is an example of a transitional word.
9. .... Concrete words describe real things that you can experience with your five senses.
10. .... Abstract words describe feelings and things that are tangible.

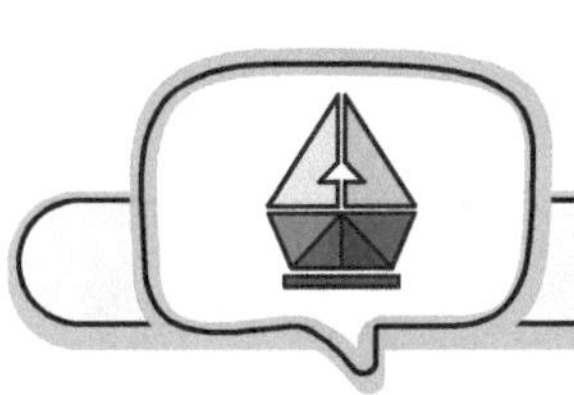

Week 10 • Activity 4

Punctuate It!

Directions: Rewrite the following sentences, adding the correct punctuation. Each sentence contains 1-3 instances of missing punctuation. An example has been done for you.

Example:

Sentence: Larry turned forty one yesterday but he didn't want a party.

With correct punctuation: Larry turned forty**-**one yesterday**,** but he didn't want a party.

1. "I hope we make it to the store before it closes" said Linda.

2. We never should have walked this far down the road we won't make it home before dark.

3. I missed you! she said and gave me a giant hug.

4. Mark Twain said it best "When in doubt, tell the truth."

5. My dogs collar fell off while he was playing in the pond.

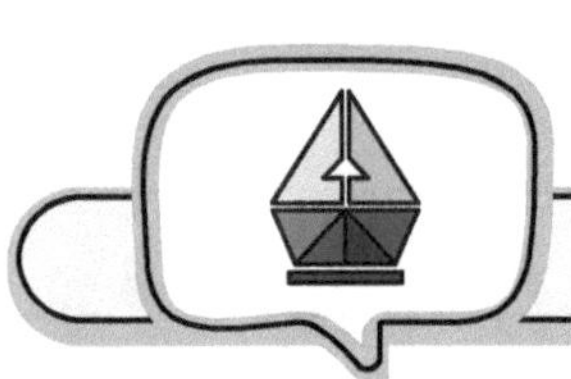

Week 10 • Activity 4

6. "Do you know what time it is" the stranger asked.

7. First you want to bring the water to a boil

8. My brother got married so now I have a new sister in law.

9. We could play baseball however the temperature has dropped dramatically and itll be cold out.

10. I have five things on my Christmas list a drum set, in line skates, a quartz necklace, a pair of earrings, a sweatshirt.

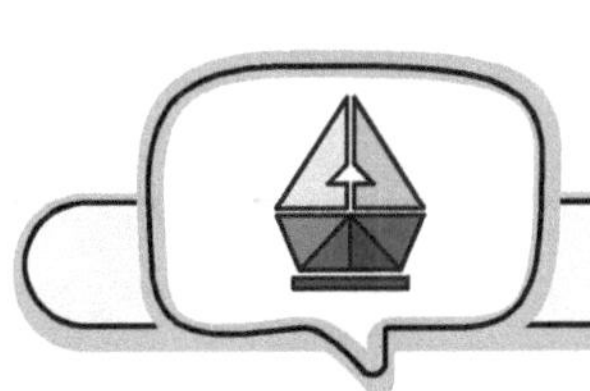

Week 10 • Activity 5

Directions: Use your imagination to write a brief conclusion as directed to end the following narrative. The first example has been done for you.

Once upon a time in the small town of Willowville, a group of curious friends named Lindsey, Colton, and Mariah discovered a mysterious old book in their school's library. The book had a worn leather cover and was filled with cryptic symbols and drawings. Excitement filled the air as the friends decided to decode the secrets hidden within its pages.

As they delved into the ancient text, the friends uncovered a map leading to the Whispering Woods, a mystical forest rumored to hold magical creatures and hidden treasures. Armed with courage and a sense of adventure, Lindsey, Colton, and Mariah set out on a journey to explore the enchanted forest.

As they ventured deeper into the Whispering Woods, the trees seemed to whisper secrets, and the air sparkled with an otherworldly glow. Suddenly, they stumbled upon a clearing where a friendly creature, half-butterfly, half-dragon, greeted them. The creature explained that the book they found held the answers that would allow them to solve the forest's riddles and unlock its true magic.

1. Write a conclusion that summarizes the main parts. (Example has been completed for you.)

In the heart of the enchanted Whispering Woods, Lindsey, Colton, and Mariah found themselves on an extraordinary adventure. Guided by a mysterious book, they uncovered a magical map leading them to the forest's secrets. Along the way, they encountered a half-butterfly, half-dragon creature, and together, they embarked on a quest to solve the riddles that guarded the forest's true magic.

2. Write a conclusion that teaches a lesson or moral.

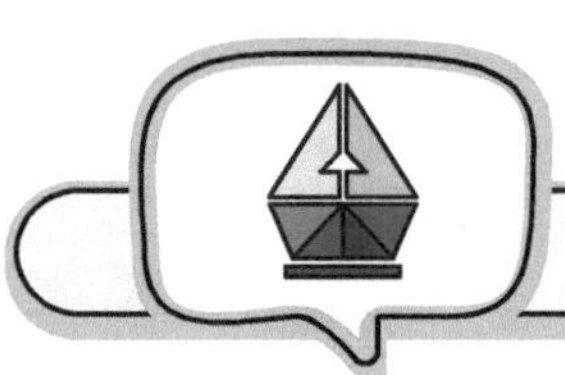

Week 10 • Activity 5

3. Write a conclusion that shares a character's thoughts and feelings.

4. Write a conclusion that ends with hope for the future.

Week 10 • Activity 6

Finding Parts

Directions: In this activity, you will underline the part of the word listed before the word. An example has been done for you.

Example: Underline the prefix in the word **post**pones.

1. Underline the suffix in the word genetic.

2. Underline the root word in the word inscribes.

3. Underline the prefix in the word understands.

4. Underline the prefix in the word mistake.

5. Underline the suffix in the word relatable.

6. Underline the root word in the word timid.

7. Underline the root word in the word senseless.

8. Underline the suffix in the word business.

9. Underline the prefix in the word substantial.

10. Underline the root word in the word inaudible.

WEEK 11

Informative Writing: Topic and Organization

After all of your learning about narrative writing, it is time to switch gears and learn how to write informative writing pieces. Informative writing pieces teach more about a topic.

ARGOPREP

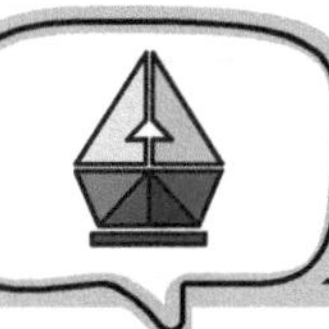

Informative Writing: Topic and Organization

This week you are going to learn about **topic** and **organization** within **informative writing**. Informative writing is writing that explains, informs, or describes something for the reader. Unlike narrative writing, which you learned about in the first half of this workbook, **informative writing** does not tell a story. Instead, **informative writing** will convey factual information.

The first thing we will learn about is how to choose a **topic** for your **informative writing** essay. A **topic** is simply what you will be giving your reader information about. Sometimes your teacher will provide you with a **topic**, but you also may be asked to choose your own **topic**. Either way, there are questions to ask yourself to help you narrow down the focus of your essay to a manageable **topic**.

Let's say you have been learning about outer space and your teacher asks you to write an informative essay about it. Outer space is a broad **topic**, so you will need to narrow it down to something specific. In order to do this, the first question you will want to ask yourself is: What do I find interesting about outer space? What do I want to learn more about? What am I skeptical of? What inspires me?

Answering these questions, you may find that you are inspired by humanity's efforts to go to Mars and skeptical about the existence of UFOs. Now you need more information about the assignment to help you choose a **topic**.

Informative writing assignments typically have specific requirements. You will be asked to use a certain number and variety of sources. We will look at sources in a later week. You will also be given a length that your essay should be, such as four pages. Finally, you need to know when your essay is due! You might think you could find five sources about Mars exploration in two weeks, but not in one week. Consider what you can do within the limits you have set for you.

Once you have your **topic** and know what information you want to provide to your audience, it's time to **organize** your essay. This week you will learn about the introductory paragraph and the body of your essay. In a later week, we will learn about writing the conclusion.

The introductory paragraph sets up the topic you are going to talk about. Good introductory paragraphs consist of three parts: an interesting hook that will grab the reader's attention, background information regarding the topic, and a thesis statement. The **thesis statement** is the most crucial part of the

entire essay and it will be last sentence in the introductory paragraph. The thesis statement is a summary of your essay and clearly states your point of view. Having a strong thesis statement will also help you **organize** the body of your essay.

Let's build a sample Introductory paragraph based on writing an essay about the existence of UFOs. The hook would be written something like this:

Are we alone in the universe, or are there other life forms observing us and possibly planning a friendly, or not-so-friendly, visit?

Next, let's provide some background information to catch the reader up to speed and inform them as to why this topic is worth reading about:

Unidentified Flying Object (UFO) sightings have been recorded ever since humanity first started recording history. Sightings have also been claimed by people on every continent in the world. Yet, no tangible evidence exists that UFOs are actually vehicles for alien life forms. Can UFO sightings be trusted, or should they be chalked up to humanity's vast imaginative abilities?

Now here is an example of a possible thesis for this essay:

By examining historical sightings, newly released government information, and recent scientific findings, the essay will show that humanity cannot yet rule out the existence of UFOs and aliens.

Now that we have a strong thesis, we can **organize** the Body of our essay. We will use our thesis statement to make that easy and logical for us and the reader. We stated in the thesis that we would specifically discuss three things: historical sightings, newly released government information, and recent scientific findings. The outline of the essay will follow these subjects in the same order they are written in the thesis statement. Here is an example of an outline for the body of the essay:

Paragraph 1: Set up the topic. Include a hook, background information, and thesis.

Thesis: By examining historical sightings, newly released government information, and recent scientific findings, the essay will show that humanity cannot yet rule out the existence of UFOs and aliens.

Paragraph 2: Discuss historical sightings of UFOs

Paragraph 3: Discuss newly released government information

Paragraph 4: Discuss recent scientific findings.

Paragraph 5: Conclusion.

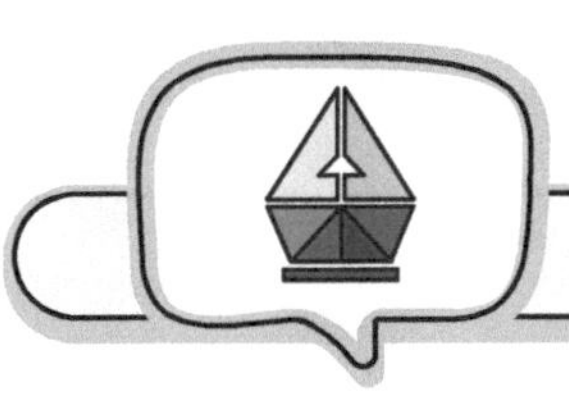

Week 11 • Activity 1

Right Answers

Directions: Answer the following questions based on what you have learned so far about writing an informative essay. An example has been done for you.

Example: What is the purpose of providing background information in the introductory paragraph?

Answer: To catch the reader up to speed and inform them why the topic is worth reading about.

1. What is the purpose of the introductory paragraph?.

Answer:

2. Once you have a broad topic, what are three questions to consider in order to help you narrow down the topic?

Answer:

3. What is the difference in informative writing and narrative writing?

Answer:

4. What is the middle part of an informative essay called?
Answer:

5. What is the most crucial part of an informative essay?
Answer:

6. What is a thesis sentence?
Answer:

7. Where is the thesis sentence written in an informative essay?
Answer:

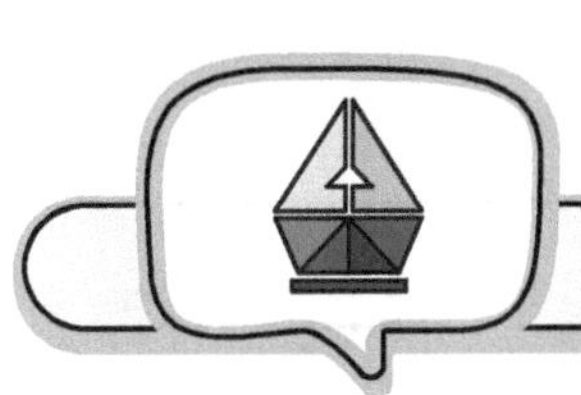

8. How do you organize information within the body paragraphs to make it clear and logical?

Answer:

....

....

....

....

9. What are three limits that you might have set for you that you should consider when choosing a topic?

Answer:

....

....

....

....

10. What is the purpose of the hook in the first paragraph of the essay?

Answer:

....

....

....

....

Brainstorm

Directions: In this activity, you will be given broad topics. The topics will be located in the center of the sun. Practice brainstorming to narrow the topic. Write your answers at the end of each of the sun's rays. An example has been done for you.

Example:

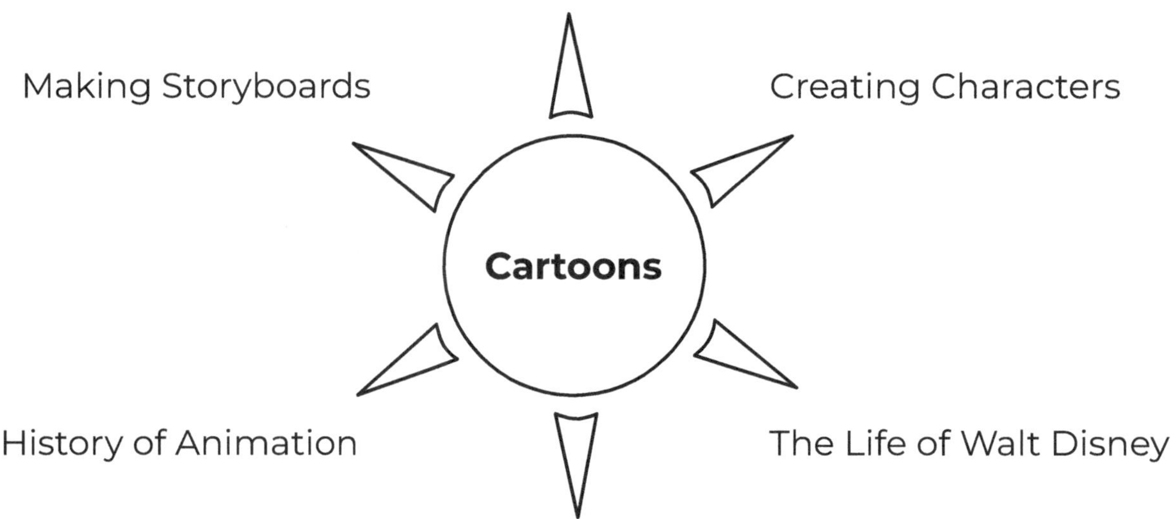

1.

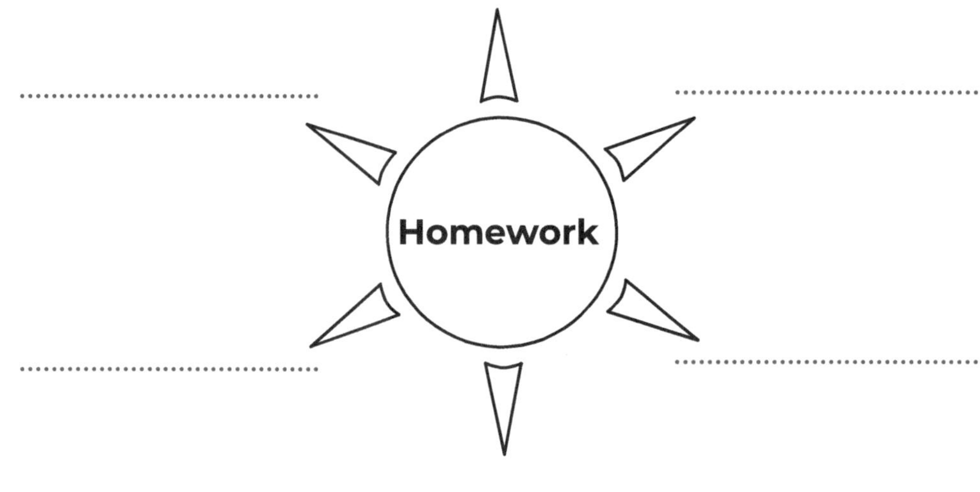

2.

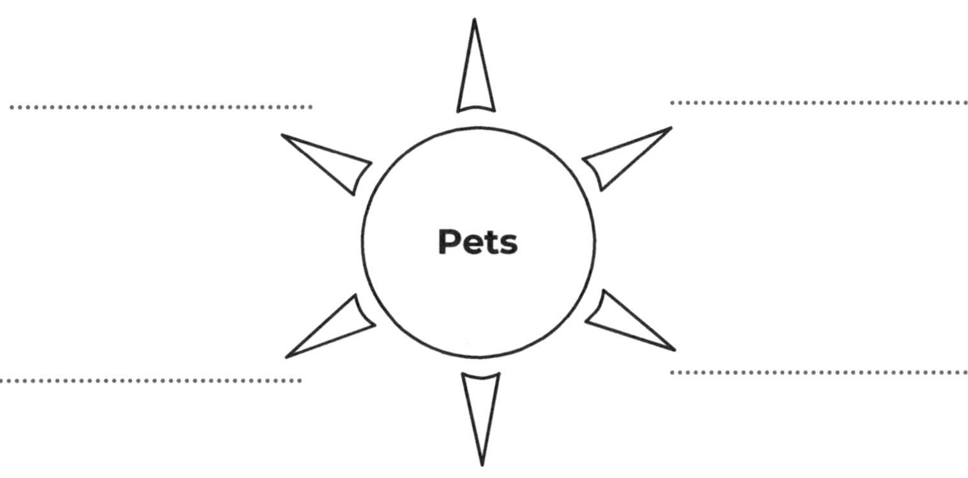

3.

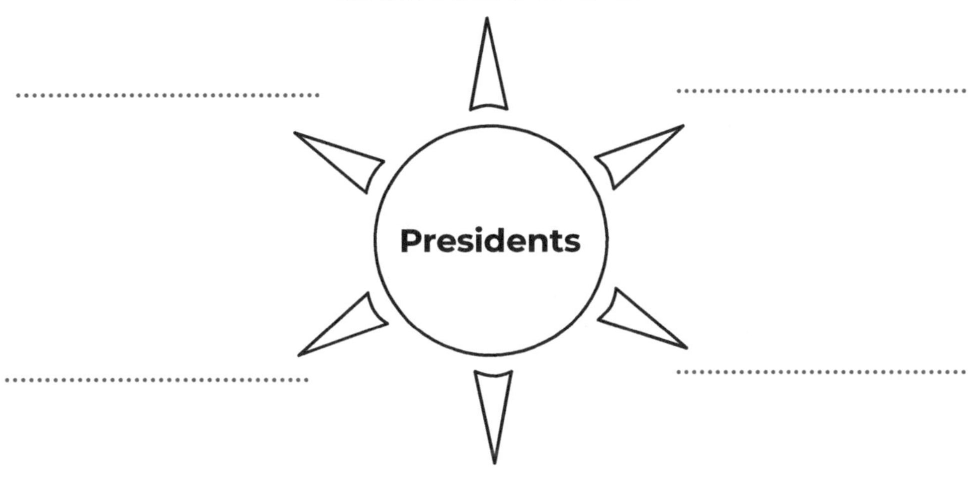

4.

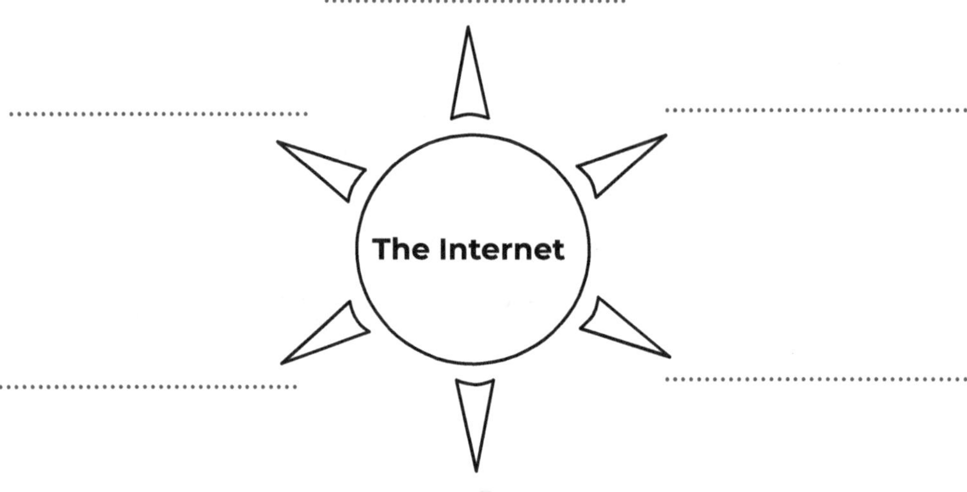

5.

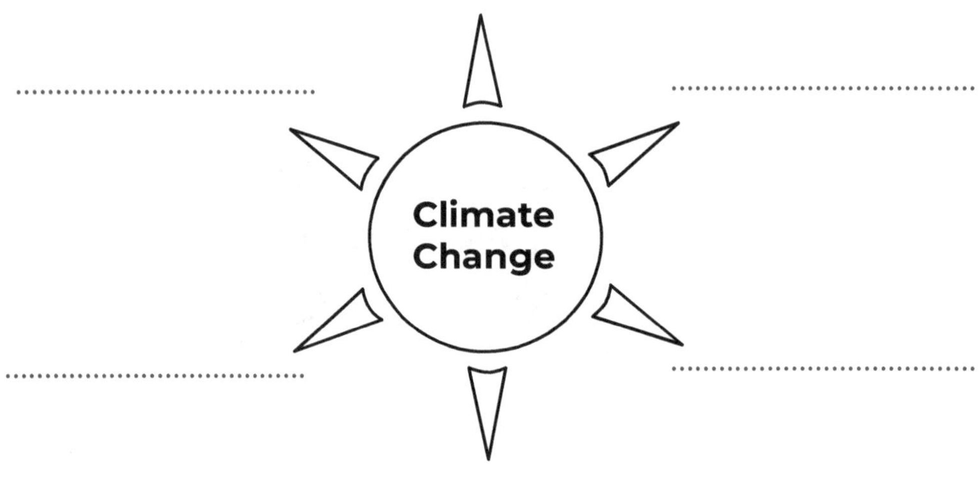

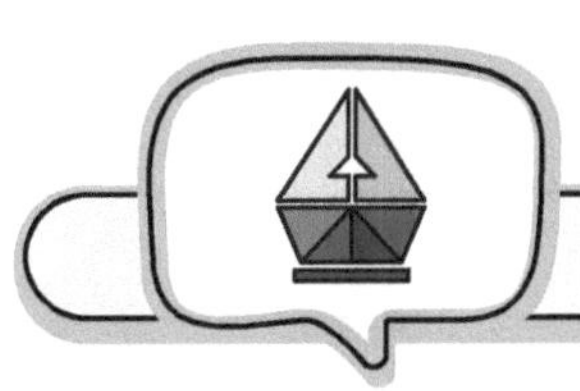

Building the Body

Directions: In this activity, you will be given a thesis statement. Outline the body of a potential essay based off of the thesis statement. An example has been done for you.

Example:

Thesis: Despite being a complex conflict, the Civil War was fundamentally fought over three issues: economic disparity between the North and South, the debate over states' rights versus federal authority, and the morality of slavery.

Body Outline:

First Paragraph of Body: The economic disparity between the North and South.

Second Paragraph of Body: The debate over states' rights versus federal authority.

Third Paragraph of Body: The morality of slavery.

1. Thesis: There are three important factors to consider when thinking about the potential for life on Mars: the geological condition of the environment, the ongoing search for evidence of life, and the potential implications for human colonization.

   Body Outline:
   First Paragraph of Body:

   ....

   ....

   ....

   Second Paragraph of Body:

   ....

   ....

   ....

Third Paragraph of Body:

2. Thesis: The wives of American Presidents have shaped the country by advising on policy, championing charitable work, and influencing the fashion industry.

   Body Outline:

   First Paragraph of Body:

   Second Paragraph of Body:

   Third Paragraph of Body:

3. Thesis: Corporations can make better environmental choices by adopting sustainable sourcing methods, implementing energy efficient technologies, and fostering transparent communication with consumers.

   Body Outline:

   First Paragraph of Body:

Second Paragraph of Body:

Third Paragraph of Body:

4. Thesis: Public libraries are important institutions in our society because of the role they play in knowledge and education, the accessibility they provide to diverse resources, and fostering a lifelong love of learning through programs and services.

Body Outline:

First Paragraph of Body:

Second Paragraph of Body:

Third Paragraph of Body:

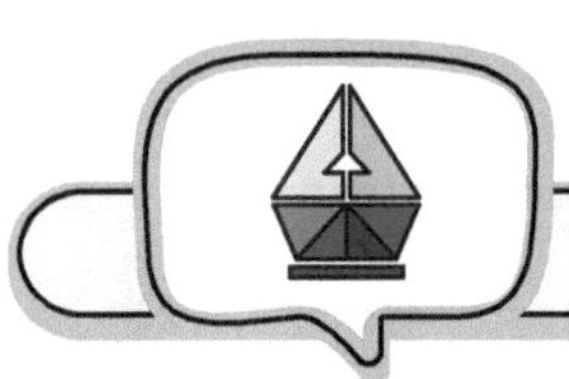

Week 11 • Activity 3

5. Thesis: The life cycles of butterflies consist of going from egg to caterpillar, metaphorizing within the chrysalis, and emerging as a beautify butterfly.

Body Outline:

First Paragraph of Body:

....

....

....

Second Paragraph of Body:

....

....

....

Third Paragraph of Body:

....

....

....

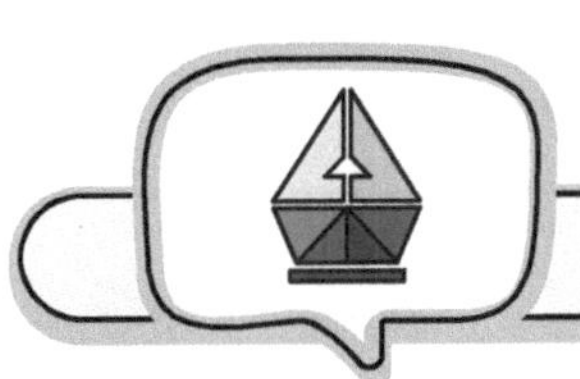

Week 11 • Activity 4

True or False

Directions: Identify each statement as True for False. In the space to the left of the statement, write a **T** if it is true and an **F** if it is false. An example has been done for you.

Example: .....T..... Informative writing is different than narrative writing.

1. .... The thesis is the most crucial part of an informative essay.

2. .... Informative essays consist of an introductory paragraph, body paragraphs, and a conclusory paragraph.

3. .... Opinions are important to include in informative writing.

4. .... A hook is used to catch the reader's attention.

5. .... The outline of an essay should follow the sequence set up in the thesis statement.

6. .... Broad topics do not need to be narrowed down.

7. .... The thesis statement will be the first sentence of your essay.

8. .... When choosing a topic, it's important to consider when your essay is due.

9. .... Asking yourself what you want to know more about is a good question to help you narrow down a topic.

10. .... You will have to use sources in informative essays.

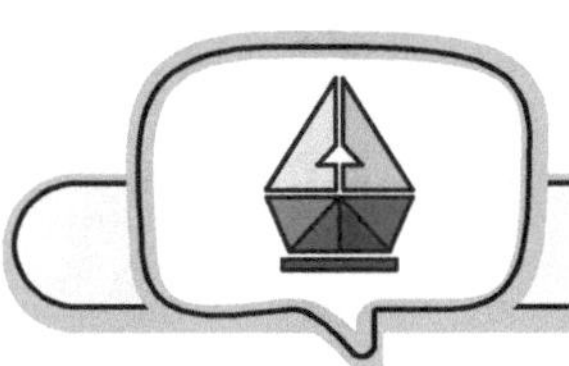

Gone Fishing

Directions: In this activity, you will be given a topic. Your task is to come up with a hook that will inspire someone to read more about the topic. An example has been done for you.

Example:

Topic: The Secret Life of Cats

Hook: You may think Mr. Whiskers naps all day while you are at school, but chances are he is going on his own wild adventures.

1. Topic: The Northern Lights
Hook:

2. Topic: Castles of England
Hook:

3. Topic: The Day in the life of an Octopus
Hook:

4. Topic: Choosing a Career
Hook:

5. Topic: The Art of Storytelling
Hook:

6. Topic: Families in the Middle Ages
Hook:

7. Topic: Hibernation of Bears
Hook:

8. Topic: Writing a Novel
Hook:

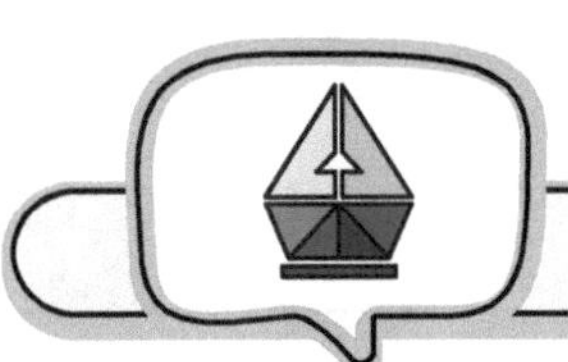

9. Topic: Popular Music

Hook:

....

....

....

10. Topic: The Four Seasons

Hook:

....

....

....

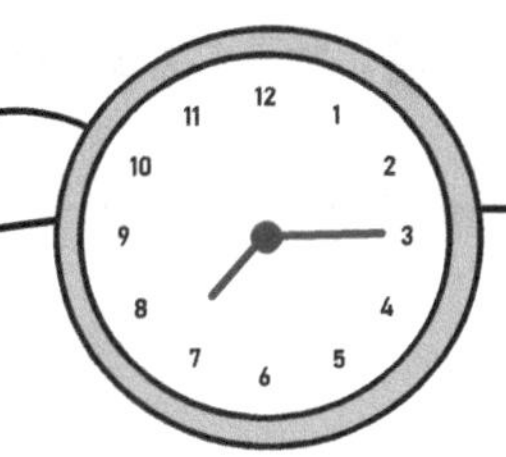

WEEK 12

Informative Writing: Facts and Details

Facts

Citations

Detail

Now that you've learned the basics of informative writing, you'll learn a little more about how to make it the best it can be.

Week 12

Informative Writing: Facts and Details

This week you are going to learn about **facts** and **details** within **informative writing**. Remember, informative writing is writing that explains, informs, or describes something for the reader. Since informative writing strives to convey accurate information, it is crucial to understand **facts** and **details** and how to include them in your essay.

When you begin to research for your essay, you will be looking for **facts** and **details** to support your main idea. Imagine that your main idea is a treasure, and the supporting **facts** are the map that helps your readers find the treasure.

Supporting **facts** are evidence that proves your point-of-view. Ask yourself, "What **details** will help people understand or believe what I'm saying?" Look for **details** that explain, describe, or give more information about your main idea.

In the world of writing, it is very important to know the difference between **facts** and opinions. **Facts** are things that can be proven true. For example, if you say, "The sun rises in the east," that is a **fact** because we can observe that happening every day.

Opinions, on the other hand, are personal feelings, thoughts, and preferences. If you say, "Chocolate ice cream is the best tasting ice cream flavor," that is your opinion and someone might disagree. If you are sharing opinions in your essay, be sure to indicate that to the reader by prefacing them with statements such as, "In my personal opinion..." or "He felt that..."

It is very important to make sure your **facts** and **details** are accurate. When researching your topic, you may come across a wonderful **fact** that will support your point-of-view. Before including it in your writing, you need to make sure it is an accurate fact. A great way to do this is by confirming the information with a variety of reliable sources.

Sources can be many things: books, articles, films, interviews, online sources, and more. A reliable source is one where you can trust the information to be accurate. Here are a few questions to ask in order to determine if a source is reliable: Is the author of the information an expert on the subject? Does the author have the education and/or training to give them knowledge about the topic? Can the information be verified by someone else who is also knowledgeable on the topic? When was the information written? Information will not always change, but it is important to make sure the information is up-to-date in fields where information is constantly evolving, such as technology, science, and medicine.

You will also be asked to cite your sources. Citations are included in order to give credit to the author and to show others where to find the information. Citations include the name of the author, the title of the work, the date of publication, and additional information. There are a few different methods for including citations in your work and your teacher will tell you which way they want this done.

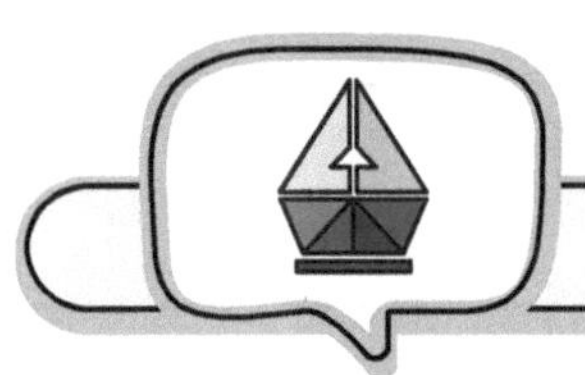

Who Knows?

Directions: Identify which of these sources would be a reliable source for the given topic. Circle all of the reliable sources. An example has been done for you.

Example:

Topic: writing a successful paper

Sources:

My English Teacher (circled)

My Little Brother

A Hockey Player

A Famous Author (circled)

Now it's your turn!

Topic: The Inner Workings of the Human Body

A Basketball Coach

A Doctor

My Sister

A Cashier

An Encyclopedia

An Online Medical Journal

TikTok

A Nurse

A Gardener's Blog

A Nutritionist

A Documentary about the Body

An Interview with a Surgeon

People Magazine

A Veterinarian

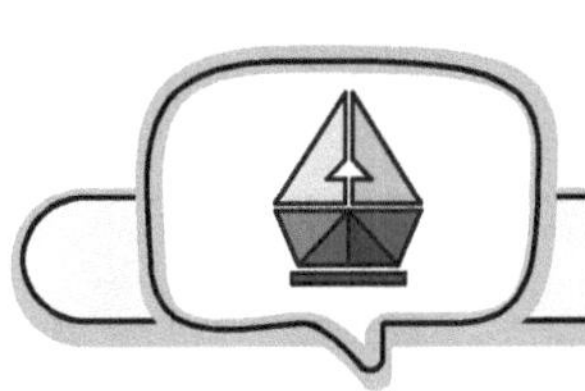

Week 12 • Activity 2

That's a Fact!

Directions: Below you will be given sets of sentences. Choose which sentence would be the stronger sentence to use in an informative essay. Mark your answer in the space provided. An example has been done for you.

Example:

.... Golden Retrievers are the most popular dog, which is evident because all of my friends have them.

.......X....... According the National Kennel Society, Golden Retrievers accounted for 25% of all dogs owned in the United States.

1. .... Many people do just fine on five hours of sleep a night.

.... Doctors recommend 7-9 hours of sleep a night.

2. .... The average lifespan of a wild panda is 15-20 years.

.... According to legend, pandas were once entirely white.

3. .... Adding sugar to spaghetti sauce can make it sweeter.

.... Italy produces 1.43 million tons of spaghetti per year.

4. .... A nosebleed occurs when a blood vessel inside of the nose bursts.

.... My uncle told me my nosebleed was nothing to be worried about.

5. .... NASCAR races are far more interesting to watch than Formula 1 races.

.... The fastest racecar in the world in the Bugatti Veyron Super Sport.

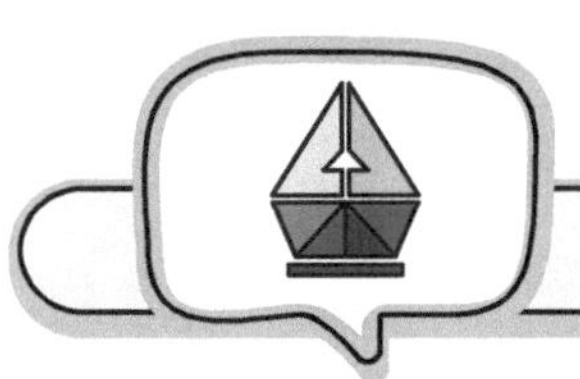

Week 12 • Activity 3

Treasure Hunt

Directions: For this activity, you will be given a thesis statement, followed by supporting facts. Underline the facts that will best support the thesis statement. An example has been done for you.

Example:

Thesis: Cooking at home not only enhances culinary skills, but can also promote healthy eating habits and create lasting family memories.

Facts:

<u>Meals made at home typically have fewer calories and more nutrition than those found at restaurants.</u>

Going through the drive-thru can be a quick and inexpensive way to feed your family after a busy day.

<u>Spending time around the table with family and friends has been linked to lower levels of depression and heart disease.</u>

Now it's your turn!

Thesis: Penguins' special physical adaptations, remarkable social behavior, and various species make the more than just cute Arctic animals.

Facts:

Penguins have flipper-like wings that serve as efficient paddles.

Penguins were called weird geese when they were discovered.

The feathers of penguins are coated with special oil that makes them waterproof.

The circulatory system of a penguin allows it to regulate its body temperature efficiently.

Penguins are native to the Southern Hemisphere.

The upright posture of penguins is crucial for activities such as nesting, socializing, and traveling across various habitats.

Empirical penguins are the largest penguin species.

I know a lot about penguins because they are my favorite animal!

Gentoo penguins are characterized by a bright orange beak and a white stripe across their head.

A group of penguins in water is called a raft.

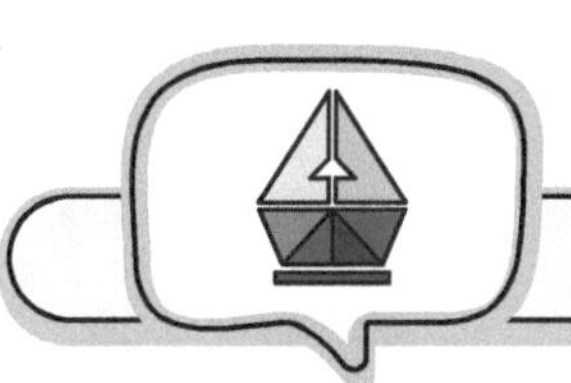

Matches

Directions: In this activity, you will choose which topic from the word bank to match each fact. Write the corresponding topic beside the fact. Not all topics will be used. An example has been done for you.

Unique Animal Diets	Vehicle Ownership
Games Around The World	History of Modern Dance
Benefits of Music	American Inventions
Life in Outer Space	Desserts from Finland
Weather Wonders	How Color Affects Us
Driving Safety	Bullying in High School

Example: Driving Safety .... Correctly used seatbelts reduce the risk of death in a crash by 61%.

1. .... Koalas eat poisonous leaves.
2. .... There is no water on the moon.
3. .... School uniforms have been shown to reduce bullying.
4. .... The hip hop dance style originated in the 1970s.
5. .... Tea bags were invented in the United States in 1904.
6. .... Although they look fluffy, clouds are not weightless.
7. .... The oldest known board game is called Senet.
8. .... Taylor Swift's favorite color is purple.
9. .... Your plants like music, too!
10. .... 95% of a car's lifetime is spent parked.

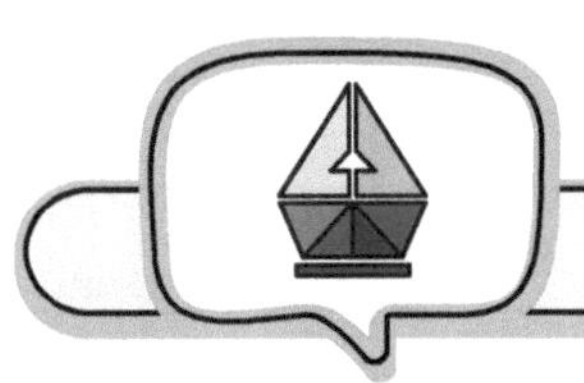

Week 12 • Activity 5

Fill in the Blank

Directions: Using what you have learned from the chapter, fill in the blanks with the appropriate word or phrase. An example has been done for you.

Example: <u>Facts</u> are things that can be proven true.

1. Facts and details are used to .... the main idea.

2. Citations should include the author of the work, the ...., and the date of publication.

3. Supporting facts are the .... that helps your readers find the treasure.

4. .... shows readers where to find the information you are using.

5. One way to tell if a source is reliable is to see if the information can be verified by another person who is an .... in the field.

6. .... are personal feelings or preferences.

7. In some fields of study, you need to know .... something was written to make sure the information is up-to-date.

8. Citations give credit to the .... of the work.

9. "In my personal opinion" and "He felt that" are statements that would precede an opinion, not a .... or a ....

10. It's very important to make sure facts are .... before including them in your essay.

WEEK 13

Word Choice: Content-Specific Vocabulary

You learned about word choice in the narrative writing section. Word choice is important in informative writing, too, but there are different things to consider.

Week 13  Word Choice: Content-Specific Vocabulary

Content-Specific Vocabulary, sometimes also called domain-specific vocabulary, refers to words and phrases specific to a subject that are rarely used outside of their particular content area. Knowing **content-specific vocabulary** is important when writing informative essays because without understanding the vocabulary associated with the subject, it is impossible to understand the information you are reading and passing along to your reader.

Have you ever been in a group of people, such as hobby enthusiasts or people in the same career, and it almost seems like they are speaking a different language? This is because they are using **content-specific vocabulary**.

For instance, if your grandmother invited you to drop in on her knitting group, she and her peers may use words and phrases that you've never heard before because and cannot understand. This doesn't mean you are any less smart, it just means that groups of people develop words and phrases for things that they encounter regularly that others may not.

The best way to learn content-specific vocabulary about a particular subject is to read things written about that subject. Look up the definitions of any words that you do not recognize. Even if you recognize the word, if the meaning doesn't seem to make sense, look up the word. It could be that the word has a different meaning that is specific only to the way it is being used within the context of the subject.

Word Choice: Content-Specific Vocabulary

To understand exactly what content-specific vocabulary is, it's helpful to think of the words placed into different tiers. Here is an example of tiers and how to determine where a word would fit on the pyramid.

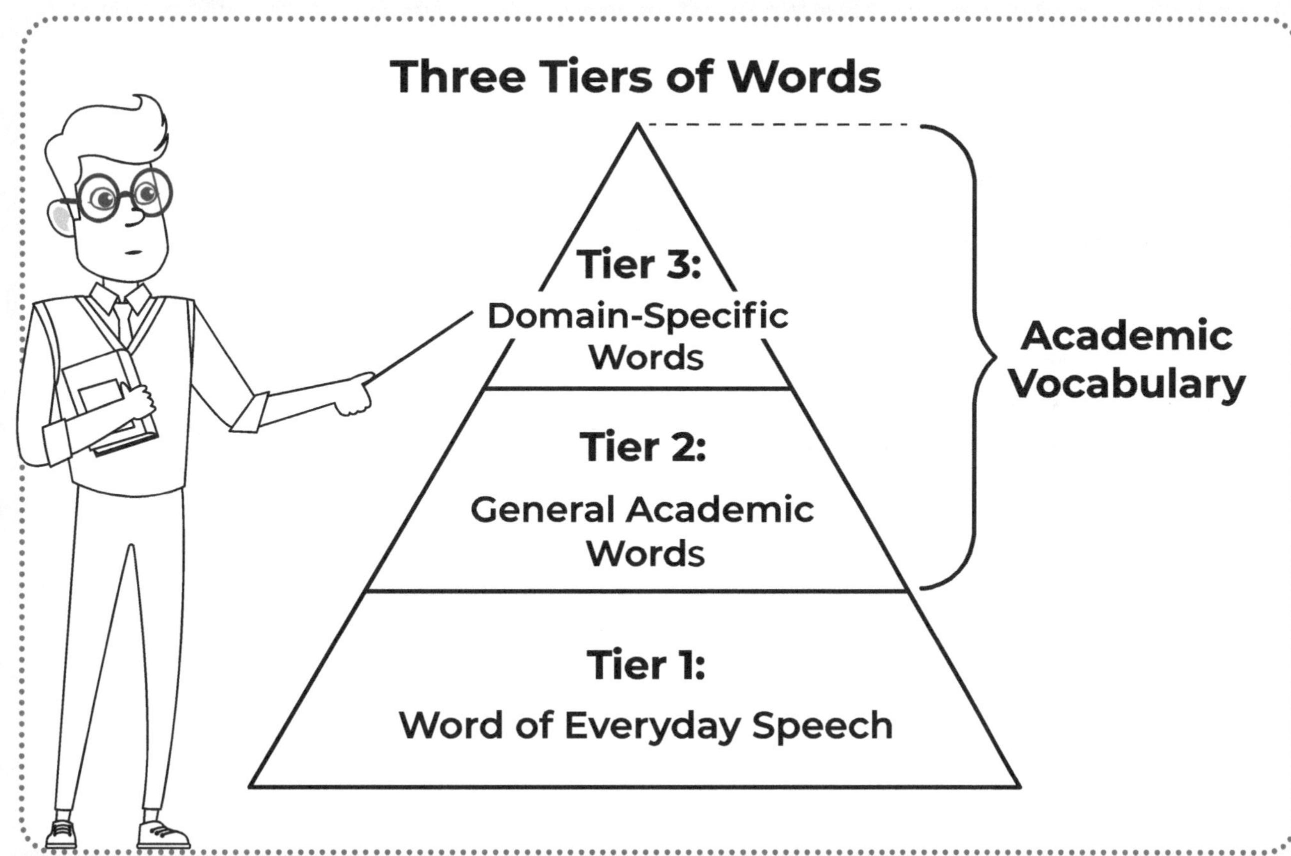

There are many other ways to learn content-specific vocabulary about subjects you are interested in, such as following experts about that subject on social media, joining groups or activities where people discuss or practice your interest, and listening to podcast related to the subject you're interested in. **Content-specific vocabulary** may seem intimidating at first, but with a little exposure you'll pick up on it in no time!

It's important to understand content-specific vocabulary about a subject when you begin to write an informative essay. Understanding content-specific vocabulary will help you grasp the meaning of what you are reading or hearing while researching. You can then clearly explain the subject to your reader and teach them some content-specific vocabulary, too!

Word Choice: Content-Specific Vocabulary

Content-Specific Vocabulary will be words found on the top tier. Let's look at an example to help you further understand this concept. This example uses words commonly associated with mathematics.

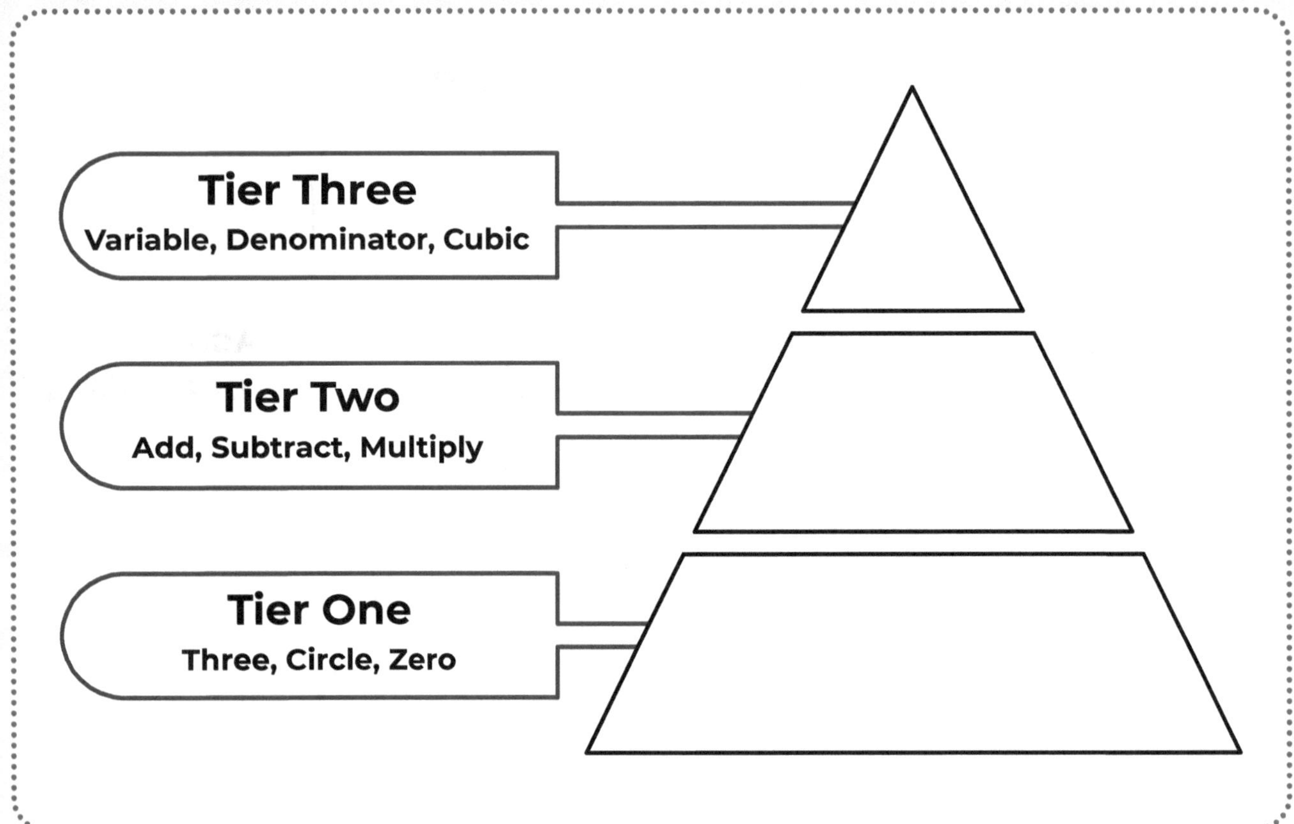

Tier one words are words that are commonly used in everyday speech. Tier two words are words that are usually used in academic settings, but can be sometimes be used across multiple subjects. Tier three words are our content-specific words, words that have specialized meanings and are only used when discussing a particular topic.

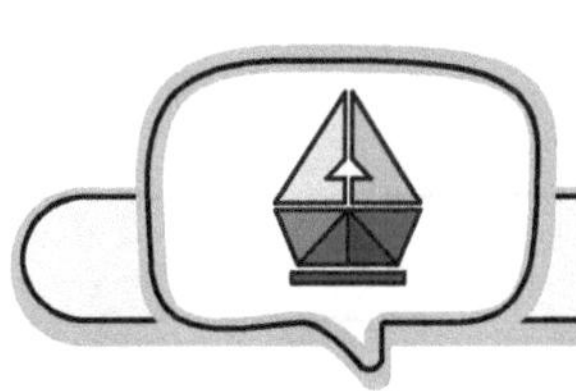

Week 13 • Activity 1

Directions: Read the following story about a cook named Olivia. Content-specific cooking vocabulary is in bold. Use what you learn about cooking to correctly match the bold word to its correct pot. Pot 1 has been filled in as an example.

In a cozy kitchen nestled between the hustle and bustle of the city, Chef Olivia embarked on a culinary adventure. With a shimmering pan in hand, she began to **deglaze** the remnants of succulent roast, coaxing out every bit of flavor from the caramelized bits. The rich aroma filled the air as she prepared to sauté a medley of fresh vegetables, expertly wielding the spatula to ensure each piece was kissed by the sizzling pan.

Next on the agenda was a fragrant garlic and herb marinade. With finesse, Olivia **minced** garlic cloves into tiny, aromatic pieces, releasing their pungent essence. She then combined the minced garlic with a blend of fresh herbs, creating a **marinade** for the roast to sit in and absorb the flavors, elevating the upcoming dish to new heights.

Turning her attention to a marbled piece of meat, Olivia decided to **sear** it to perfection. The pan crackled with excitement as she placed the meat, allowing it to develop a golden crust that would lock in its juices. The **searing** process unleashed a symphony of sizzles, creating an appetizing melody that hinted at the deliciousness to come.

As the main course began to take shape, Olivia zestfully added a burst of citrus to the mix. Using a zester, she extracted the vibrant oils from an orange, infusing the dish with a lively and refreshing note. The aroma of the **zest** mingled with the savory scents, creating an enticing fusion of flavors.

With the stage set, Chef Olivia carefully transferred the ingredients to a pot, where they would simmer to perfection. The **simmering** process allowed the flavors to meld together, creating a harmonious dance that transformed individual elements into a cohesive masterpiece. As the kitchen filled with the tantalizing aroma of the simmering concoction, Olivia couldn't help but smile, knowing that her culinary creation was about to delight the senses.

Week 13 • Activity 1

Pot 1

The process of locking in a meat's juices.

Pot 4

A combination of herbs that will be absorbed by the food.

Pot 2

To coax out the flavor of carmalezid bits left in a pan.

Pot 5

To chop into tiny pieces.

Pot 3

To extract oils from an orange or other citrus fruit.

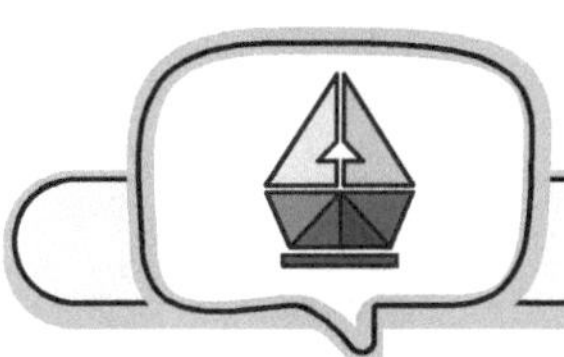

Week 13 • Activity 2

Directions: Read the following short story about dance, paying close attention to content-specific vocabulary. Underline at least two tier one words, highlight at least two tier two words, and circle at least two tier three words.

In the lively town of Harmonyville, there was a young girl named Sabrina who had a deep passion for dance. Sabrina loved to twirl and spin, letting the music guide her every move. One day, her dance teacher, Mrs. Miller, introduced the class to the enchanting world of choreography. They learned how to create beautiful routines, combining different steps and movements to the rhythm of the music.

In their dance class, Sabrina discovered the joy of performing a pirouette – a graceful spin on one foot. With determination and practice, she perfected this elegant move, feeling a sense of accomplishment. Mrs. Miller taught them about various dance styles, and Sabrina was particularly fascinated by the tango, a dance that required precise footwork and partner coordination.

As Sabrina and her classmates continued to learn and practice, the recital day arrived. The stage was set, and the excitement filled the air. Sabrina and her friends showcased their carefully crafted choreography, incorporating spins, twirls, and even the mesmerizing pirouette. The audience clapped and cheered as they witnessed the young dancers bringing the magic of rhythm and movement to life.

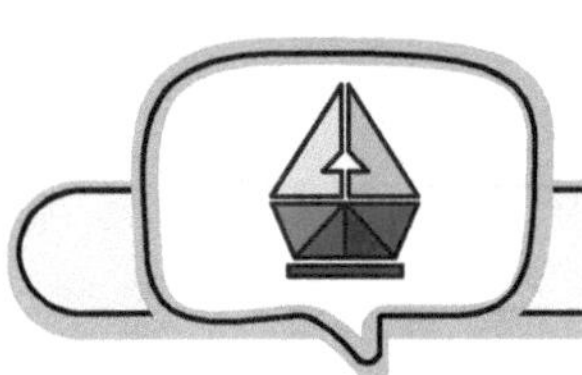

Week 13 • Activity 3

It'll Have You in Tiers

Directions: In this activity, you will place words from a word bank into the correct tier. Remember, Tier 1 words are commonly used in everyday speech, Tier 2 words are less commonly used but can still be applied to different subjects, and Tier 3 words are content-specific, highly specialized language. An example for each Tier has been done for you.

Sports Word Bank

Run	Equestrian	Athlete
Championship	Dribble	Play
Homerun	Win	Drop Shot
Teamwork	Coach	Lose

Tier 3 Words: Dribble

Tier 2 Words: Teamwork

Tier 1 Words: Win

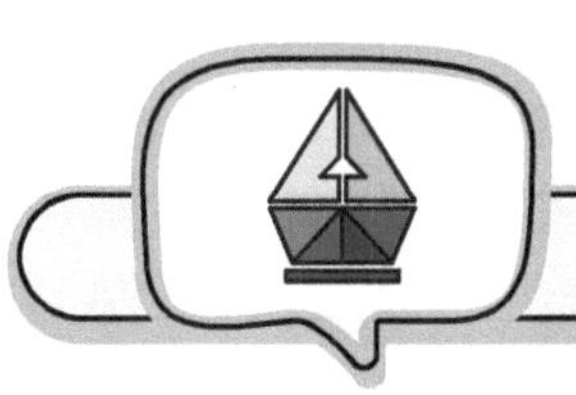

Week 13 • Activity 4

Q & A

Directions: Answer the following questions based off of what you have learned in this chapter. An example has been done for you.

Example:

Question: What would be a tier two word associated with science?

Answer: Investigate

1. Question: What is the best way to learn content-specific vocabulary?
   Answer:

2. Question: Why is understanding content-specific vocabulary important?
   Answer:

3. Question: What kind of words are found in tier one?
   Answer:

4. Question: How can you tell the difference between a tier two word and a tier three word?
   Answer:

5. Question: What are some additional ways you can learn content-specific vocabulary?
   Answer:

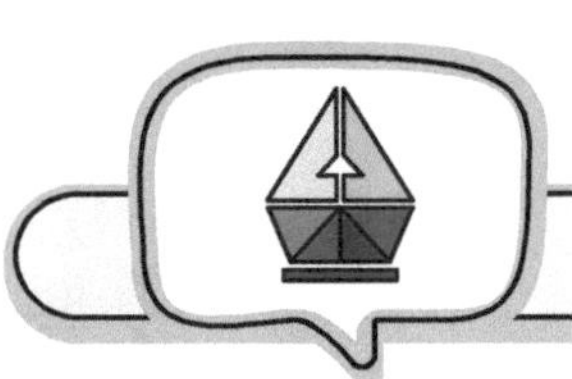

Week 13 • Activity 5

You're the Expert!

Directions: For this activity, you get to choose the topic. Pick something that you know a lot about and/or enjoying doing. Then come up with lists of tier words or phrases for that topic. Include at least five words for each tier. An example has been done for you.

Example:

Topic: Creative Writing

Tier 1 Words: Character, Hero, Style, Grammar, Hero

Tier 2 Words: Plot, Fiction, Flashback, Irony, Epiphany

Tier 3 Words: Manuscript, Query Letter, Exposition, Nonlinear narrative, Denouement

Now it's your turn!

Topic:

Tier 1 Words:

Tier 2 Words:

Tier 3 Words:

WEEK 14

Informative Writing: Transitions and Conclusions

Just like narrative writing, informative writing should have transitions and conclusions. This week, you'll learn about how to write strong transitions and conclusions in informative writing.

Informative Writing: Transitions and Conclusions

So far you have learned about how to choose a topic for your informative writing essay, how to choose facts and details to include, and how to organize the information. Now it's time to learn about **transitions** and **conclusions**.

Transitions are words or phrases that will improve the flow of your writing. **Transitions** help link together ideas, sentences, and paragraphs. They show relationships that help readers understand the thoughts, concepts, and flow of the essay. **Transitions** may connect, contrast, show cause and effect, indicate order, and accomplish other associations.

The following table gives some examples of **transition** words and phrases and when to use them.

Transition Words and Phrases	When to Use Them
* In my opinion * She believes * Their favorite	Stating an opinion
* Since * Next * Another reason	Linking ideas or paragraphs
* For example * Additionally * In fact	Providing examples/details
* In conclusion * Finally * To summarize	Coming to a conclusion

Informative Writing: Transitions and Conclusions

The **Conclusion** is the final paragraph of the essay. The **Conclusion** paragraph wraps everything up and signals to the reader that the essay is ending. The **Conclusion** focuses on the big ideas of the essay, not minor details, and brings everything together.

The first sentence of the conclusion should be your thesis statement reworded. Remember, your thesis was the last sentence of your first paragraph and stated what would be discussed in the essay.

No new ideas are introduced in the **conclusion**, but this is where you can address limitations or include a call to action. A call to action is where you ask your readers to take the next step in learning more about the topic or putting what they have learned into action.

Finally, it's important to have a strong closing sentence. The closing sentence will be the last sentence of your paper. This is the reader's last impression of your topic and it should leave a lasting impression.

To recap how an essay is organized and what the purpose of each section is, let's look again at the simple three steps you learned in Week Eleven. Your essay should be arranged in the following way:

Tell what you're going to tell them (**introduction**).

Tell them (**body**).

Tell them what you told them (**conclusion**).

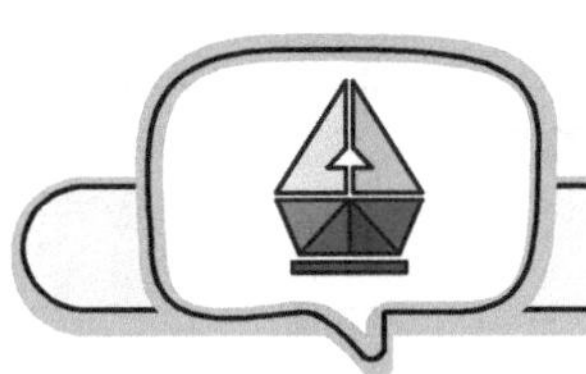

Week 14 • Activity 1

Smooth Transitions

Directions: For this activity, fill in the column with appropriate transition words or phrases. Try to get at least four and be sure they are different from the ones in the lesson's table. An example has been completed for you.

Transition Words and Phrases	When to Use Them
Example: In my view	Stating an opinion
	Linking ideas or paragraphs
	Providing examples/details
	Coming to a conclusion

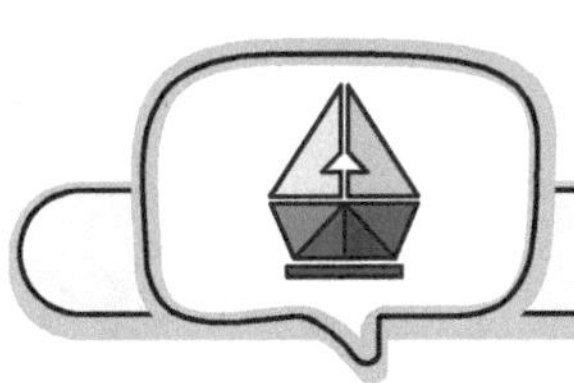

Word Hunt

Directions: Read the following story and find all of the transitional words or phrases used and highlight them. An example has been done for you.

Dragons have captured the imaginations of people across cultures and centuries, transcending mere folklore to become iconic symbols in mythology and literature. These mythical creatures, often depicted as large, fire-breathing reptiles with formidable scales and wings, have endured as fascinating entities that symbolize power, mystery, and magic. **In this writer's opinion**, dragons are the most complex and intriguing supernatural being to ever grace literature.

To begin with, dragons have been a ubiquitous presence in various mythologies worldwide. From the benevolent Eastern dragons of Chinese folklore to the fearsome European dragons guarding treasures in medieval tales, these creatures have taken on diverse roles. In many cultures, dragons are seen as guardians of wisdom and bringers of good fortune, while in others, they are depicted as adversaries that heroes must overcome. Moreover, their versatility in cultural representation adds to the allure and intrigue surrounding dragons.

In literature, dragons have played pivotal roles in countless epic stories, becoming central figures in both classic and modern tales. Furthermore, authors have skillfully crafted narratives where dragons serve as metaphors for inner conflicts or external challenges that characters must confront. These mythical beasts embody the fantastical elements that make literature a captivating realm, where imagination knows no bounds.

The enduring popularity of dragons is evident in the entertainment industry, where movies, television shows, and video games continue to showcase these creatures in various forms. In addition, the visual spectacle of dragons brought to life through advanced CGI technology has elevated their presence on screen, captivating audiences with their majestic flights and awe-inspiring abilities. The magical allure of dragons continues to captivate audiences of all ages, transcending generations and cultural boundaries.

In conclusion, dragons remain captivating symbols that have left an indelible mark on human creativity and storytelling. To sum up, whether portrayed as mythical guardians, formidable foes, or complex characters, dragons hold a timeless fascination that persists across different mediums and cultural contexts. These majestic creatures continue to soar through the realms of human imagination, adding a touch of magic to the tapestry of myth and legend.

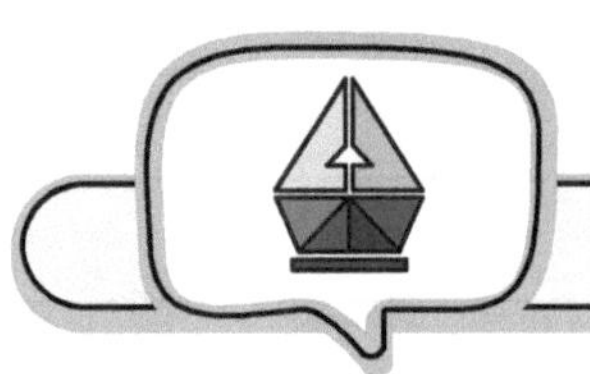

Week 14 • Activity 3

Choose the Right Transition

Directions: Fill in the blanks of the following sentences using the best transition for the word bank. An example has been done for you.

Transition Words and Phrases

In other words	Therefore	In the meantime
Next	For example	First
I feel	In conclusion	In my view
Recently	As a result	They suggest

Example: My mother and brother went to the movies. In the meantime, my dad and I built a birdhouse.

1. It's getting very late. .... like this would be the perfect time for a midnight snack.

2. The New Year is a good time to pick up healthy habits. ...., many people choose to join a gym on New Year's Day.

3. We have had very cold days lately. Most ...., the temperature reached -5 degrees.

4. ...., we had a great time at the amusement park!

5. Doctors are adamant that a good night's sleep is beneficial. .... you go to bed before 10:00 p.m.

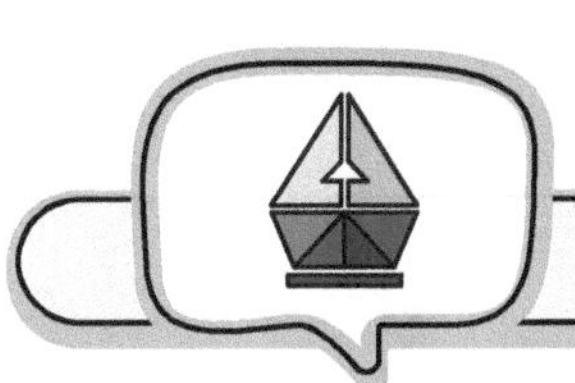

Week 14 • Activity 3

6. We will need a tent, sleeping bags, backpacks, and cooking utensils before we can go camping. ...., we have a lot of shopping to do!

7. I never studied for my exam. ...., I failed and have to retake the class.

8. Teachers have a lot of ways to tell if your homework isn't your own. ...., you should never underestimate their ability to catch you cheating.

9. Some people prefer dogs to cats. ...., cats make better pets than dogs.

10. There are two things you need to do before vigorously exercising. ...., you should warm up your muscles. ...., you should stretch.

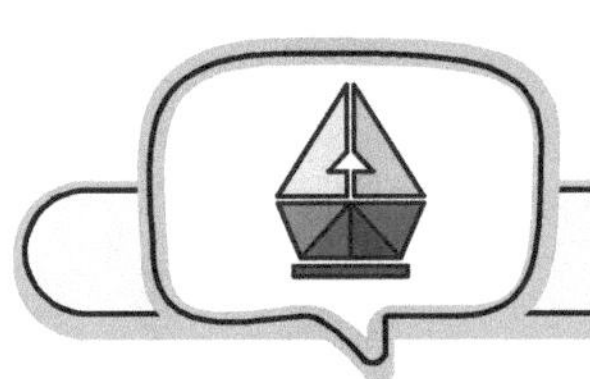

Spitball Ending

Directions: Read the following essay. The conclusion has been left off. Your job is to write the conclusion. Be sure your first sentence is the thesis reworded. An example has been done for you following the essay.

The moon landing is one of the most thrilling adventures in the history of space exploration. In 1969, astronauts Neil Armstrong and Buzz Aldrin took a giant leap for humankind by landing on the moon, and their journey is filled with incredible stories and discoveries. The moon landing has made an incomparable impact on history, science, and the human spirit.

Firstly, the moon landing was a historic event that happened on July 20, 1969. Astronauts Neil Armstrong and Buzz Aldrin traveled in a spacecraft called Apollo 11. Their mission was to explore the moon's surface and collect valuable information about our closest celestial neighbor. The whole world watched in awe as Armstrong stepped onto the moon's surface, saying the famous words, "That's one small step for man, one giant leap for mankind."

Secondly, the astronauts brought special tools and instruments to study the moon. They collected rocks and soil samples to learn more about the moon's composition. The information they gathered helped scientists understand the moon's history and how it was formed. Imagine being the first person to touch the moon's surface and bring back pieces of it to share with everyone on Earth!

Lastly, the moon landing inspired people to dream big and reach for the stars. Seeing astronauts walk on the moon showed us that with hard work, dedication, and teamwork, we can achieve incredible things. The moon landing sparked an interest in space exploration and encouraged kids like us to dream about becoming astronauts, scientists, or engineers who explore the mysteries of the universe.

Example:

In conclusion, the moon landing has had an unparalleled influence on history, science and the human ambition. The moon landing was an amazing adventure that brought people together and showed us the wonders of space. Neil Armstrong, Buzz Aldrin, and the Apollo 11 mission inspired generations to believe in the power of science and exploration. As we gaze at the moon in the night sky, we can remember the exciting day when humans first set foot on its surface, marking a giant leap for all of us.

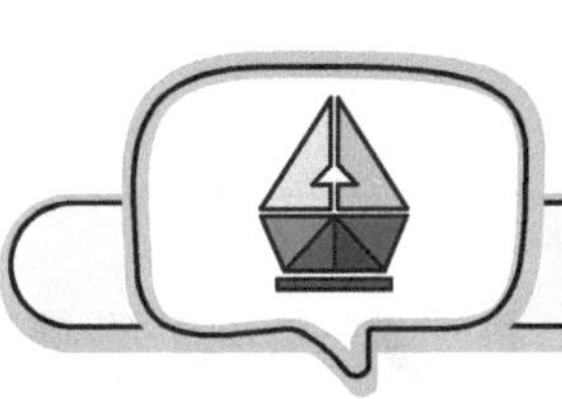

Week 14 • Activity 4

Now it's your turn! Write a conclusion.

WEEK 15

Synonyms and Antonyms

Antonym

Synonym

This week, we'll get back into looking at types of words. You'll learn about two types of words - synonyms and antonyms.

Synonyms and Antonyms

This week, you are going to learn about **synonyms** and **antonyms**. **Synonyms** are words that have a similar meaning to other words, while **antonyms** are words that mean the opposite. For example;

While standing next to the **hot** fire, you feel **warm**, not **cold**.

In this example, **hot** and **warm** are **synonyms**, while **hot** and **cold** are **antonyms**.

Using synonyms lets you **compare** using words with the **same** or **similar** meanings.

The dog was **soft** and **fluffy**.

I like the **sugary** candy because of how **sweet** it is.

Using antonyms lets you **contrast** using different words with **different** or **opposite** meanings.

The athlete was **strong**, not **weak**.

If I can't hear the **quiet** music, I can make the volume **loud**.

These activities will help you practice synonyms and antonyms.

Antonym

Cold	Hot

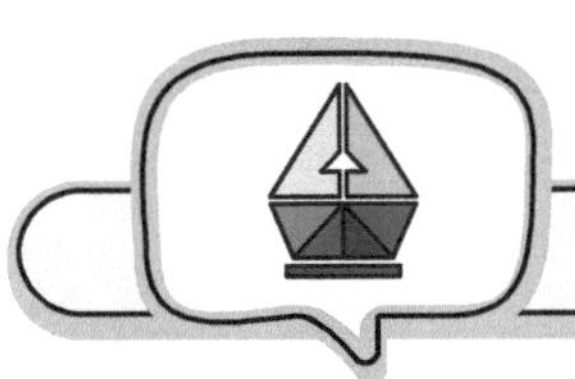

Week 15 • Activity 1

Directions: Circle the words that are **synonyms** to the word at the top.

Example: Dirty

Clean **Dusty**
Sparkling Dreary
Muddy New

1. Fast

Old Dark
Quick Speedy
Far Rapid

2. Shine

Beam Glow
Plug Close
Read Sparkle

Directions: Circle the words that are **antonyms** to the word at the top.

Example: Dirty

Clean Dusty
Sparkling Dreary
Muddy New

3. Soft

Clear Sharp
Hard Sweet
Warm Rough

4. Stop

Go Drink
Start Begin
Hold Break

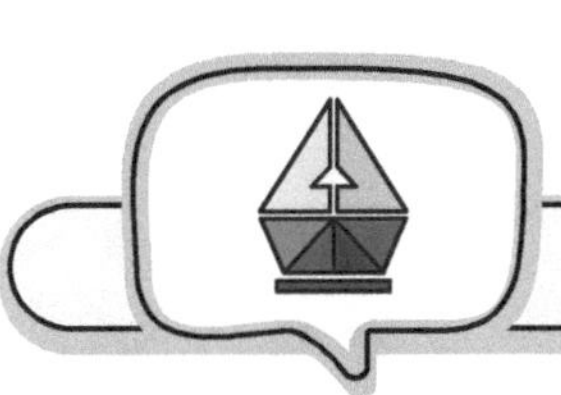

Week 15 • Activity 2

Directions: Choose if the pairs of words are **synonyms** or **antonyms**.

Example:

Dirty	Muddy	synonyms
1. Stretchy	Rubbery	....
2. Long	Short	....
3. Old	Ancient	....
4. Bright	Shiny	....
5. Open	Close	....
6. Yell	Shout	....
7. Morning	Night	....
8. Early	Late	....
9. Good	Bad	....
10. Awesome	Amazing	....

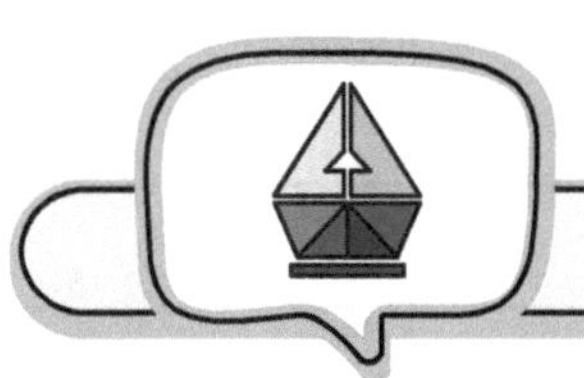

Week 15 • Activity 3

Directions: Choose the **synonym** for the underlined word.

Example:

My grandma told me to clean my <u>dirty</u> room.

A. messy **B.** tidy **C.** small **D.** clean

1. In the winter, my hands are <u>chilly</u> without gloves.

A. bad **B.** hard **C.** nice **D.** cold

2. The crayons in the box are very <u>vivid</u>.

A. pale **B.** soft **C.** colorful **D.** cool

3. I can't see the black cat in the <u>shadowy</u> night.

A. dark **B.** loud **C.** free **D.** fixed

4. Riding my bike fast makes me feel like I can <u>soar</u>.

A. crawl **B.** sit **C.** fly **D.** sleep

5. When it gets too late at night, I feel <u>tired</u>.

A. old **B.** sleepy **C.** loud **D.** happy

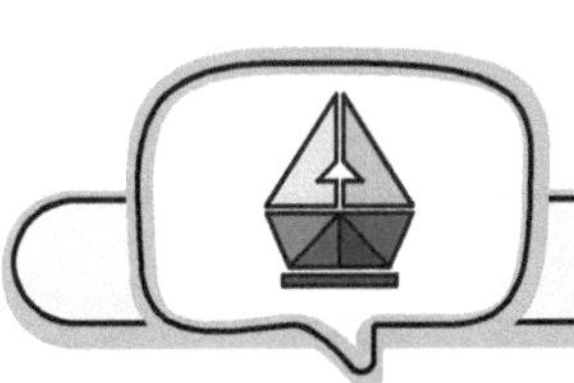

Week 15 • Activity 4

Directions: Draw a line from the word in the first column to its **antonym** in the second.

Example:

Dirty	Big
Small	Clean

Mean	Pale
Happy	Clear
Sweet	Quiet
Loud	Nice
Dark	Sour
Smile	Frown
Foggy	Sad

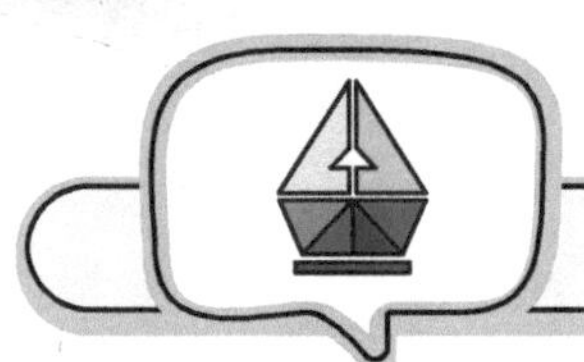

Week 15 • Activity 5

Directions: Fill in the blank with a word you know that's a **synonym** or **antonym** of the word underlined.

Example:

(ANTONYM) The cookies my dad makes are so <u>soft</u>, but when my mom makes them, they're really <u>hard</u>.

1. (ANTONYM) The movie wasn't <u>long</u> enough, and when it was over, I said it was too ....
2. (SYNONYM) My friend is very <u>silly</u>, and I always laugh when she says something ....
3. (SYNONYM) The table is <u>smooth</u> on top, so when I touch it, I can feel how .... it is.
4. (ANTONYM) The <u>young</u> puppy isn't .... enough to learn tricks.

WEEK 16

Argumentative Writing: Precise Claims and Organization

To wrap up your fourth grade writing journey, you'll learn about one more type of writing: argumentative writing.

Week 16

Argumentative Writing: Precise Claims and Organization

This week, you will learn about argumentative writing. **Argumentative writing** is writing that communicates a point of view or opinion to the reader. With argumentative writing, you **provide facts and evidence** about your side of the topic. To do this, you will want to establish your reasons and evidence logically, which you may remember from your informative writing lesson. Argumentative writing is similar—you must obtain evidence and present it in a way that makes sense, and also to convince your reader about your side of the argument.

Argumentative writing does not always need to be about whether something is true or false. Argumentative writing can be about your opinion. The important thing is getting sources together to create the argument, as well as using precise language to get your point across.

The first step in argumentative writing is selecting a topic. Selecting something that means a lot to you, like a sports team, movie, book, or game, can help make your writing stronger.

For example, you may want to argue that a basketball team is better than a different basketball team.

Next, you build your argument by selecting your points, or reasons, that support your argument.

For example, you may look at the win-loss record of the basketball team. If your team has more wins than another, that could be a **supporting point**. Be sure to have more than one supporting point, and make sure you have sources to back up your claim. Each point should have its own paragraph with the reason, sources, and opinions.

Next, you may want to look at a counterpoint, which is a reason the other side of the argument might have for thinking differently.

For example, the other team may have more well-known players. By mentioning this, you acknowledge that the other side of the argument has their own points, and you can also give your own reason why you disagree. Remember to always be polite! Your disagreement should never make the other side of the argument feel bad.

Finally, you summarize your points to conclude your argument.

In the following activities, you will work on building your argument.

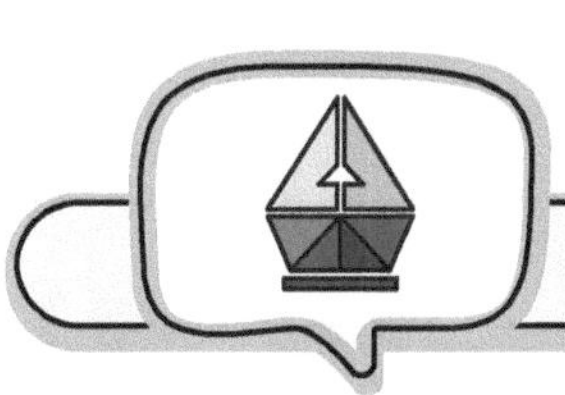

Week 16 • Activity 1

Directions: Write down five topics that you think you could write argumentatively about. Then, write what your side of the argument is, and what the other side of the argument could be.

Example:

Topic: The Wolverines are the best basketball team.

Sides: The Weasels are the best basketball team.

1. Topic: ....

   ....

   Sides: ....

   ....

2. Topic: ....

   ....

   Sides: ....

   ....

3. Topic: ....

   ....

   Sides: ....

   ....

4. Topic: ....

   ....

   Sides: ....

   ....

5. Topic: ....

   ....

   Sides: ....

   ....

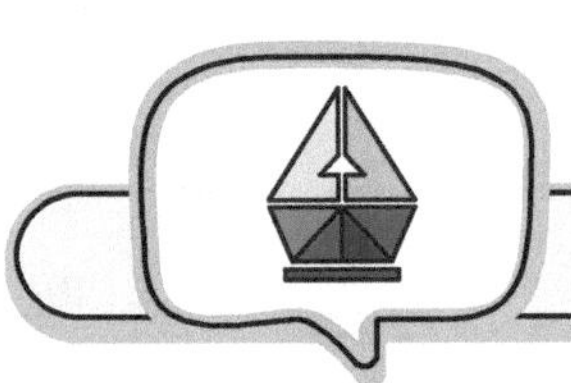

Week 16 • Activity 2

Directions: Using the same topics from Activity 1, write three supporting reasons for your argument for each topic.

Example:

Topic: The Wolverines are the best basketball team.

Reason 1: They win lots of games.

Reason 2: Their defense is strong.

Reason 3: They have a nice stadium.

1. Topic: ....

....

Reason 1: ....

....

Reason 2: ....

....

Reason 3: ....

....

2. Topic: ....

....

Reason 1: ....

....

Reason 2: ....

....

Reason 3: ....

....

3. Topic: ....

....

Reason 1: ....

....

Reason 2: ....

....

Reason 3: ....

....

4. Topic: ....

....

Reason 1: ....

....

Reason 2: ....

....

Reason 3: ....

....

5. Topic: ....

....

Reason 1: ....

....

Reason 2: ....

....

Reason 3: ....

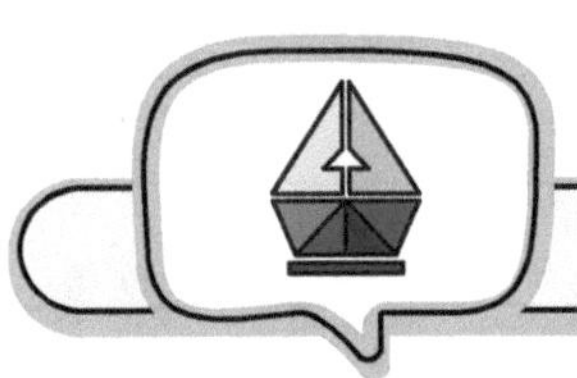

Week 16 • Activity 3

Directions: With the same topics, list one reason the other side might have for their own argument.

Example:

Topic: The Weasels are the best basketball team.

Sides: The Weasels have a offensive strategy.

1. Topic: ....

Reason : ....

2. Topic: ....

Reason : ....

3. Topic: ....

Reason : ....

4. Topic: ....

Reason : ....

5. Topic: ....

....

Reason : ....

....

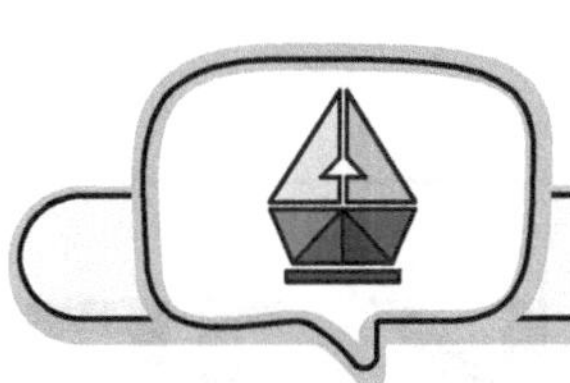

Week 16 • Activity 4

Directions: Write your own reason for disagreeing with the counterpoints stated above.

Example:

Topic: The Wolverines are the best basketball team.

Sides: The Weasels offensive is not as good as the Wolverines defense.

1. Topic: ....

Reason : ....

2. Topic: ....

Reason : ....

3. Topic: ....

Reason : ....

4. Topic: ....

Reason : ....

5. Topic: ....

....

Reason : ....

....

WEEK 17

Word Choice: Precise Language and Specific Vocabulary

Just like in narrative and informative writing, word choice matters in argumentative writing! This week, you'll explore how to choose the best words for your writing.

Word Choice: Precise Language and Specific Vocabulary

When writing argumentatively, it's important to use words that help you **communicate your meaning**, as well as words that relate to your topic. If you're writing about music, you wouldn't want to include words that talk about how the music looks. When you mention your reasons and evidence, keep in mind what your overall point is in your argument.

Think about a potential topic for an argumentative essay. Just because some words and phrases can describe the topic, that doesn't mean they're important to the argument you're trying to make. To stay on track, it can help to think about the specific points you're trying to make, and write down points that don't make sense, so that you don't include them. If you're arguing that a movie is good, your snacks at the theater probably aren't as important as the story of the movie.

Additionally, when arguing that something is good or better than something else, be sure to use words that convey goodness when talking about it. Focus on what characteristics make sense in your argument. An argument about a track star should include words that relate to what makes a track athlete a star; speed!

This is a good time to think back on your lesson on synonyms and antonyms, too. How many words can you think of that are similar to speed?

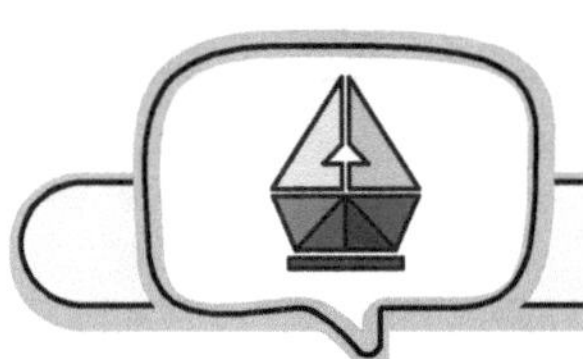

Week 17 • Activity 1

Directions: For each topic, choose the phrase that does not belong in the argument.

1. The Bears baseball team is better than the Wolves.

   A. The Bears score more points
   B. The Bears have more famous players
   C. The snacks at the game are delicious

2. The play about the kingdom is very good.

   A. The line at the theater isn't long
   B. The music sounds beautiful
   C. The actors are very engaging

3. Milk should go in the bowl before cereal.

   A. The cereal won't get so soggy
   B. Fruity cereal tastes good
   C. The milk stays cool

4. Pizza is better with fewer toppings.

   A. Breadsticks are a good appetizer
   B. Pizza should have more cheese
   C. More toppings means the pizza slice gets heavy

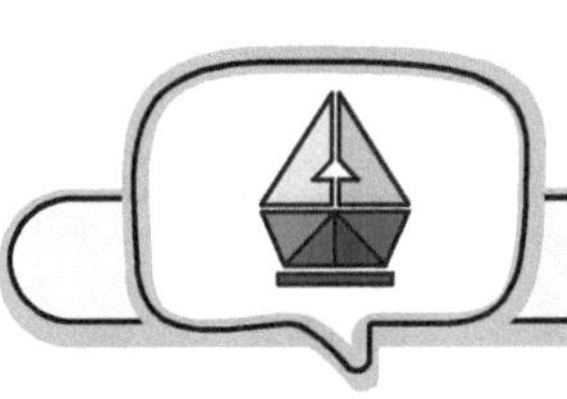

Week 17 • Activity 2

Directions: Rewrite the sentence with a word that supports the argument topic. Think about words you'd use to describe the subject that make a stronger argument than the word "best".

Example:

Video games are the best. Video games are the most fun thing to do in your free time.

1. The volleyball player on the home team is the best.

2. The chocolate chip cookie is the best.

3. Golden Retriever puppies are the best.

4. The beach in the summer is the best.

5. Building snowmen is the best part of winter.

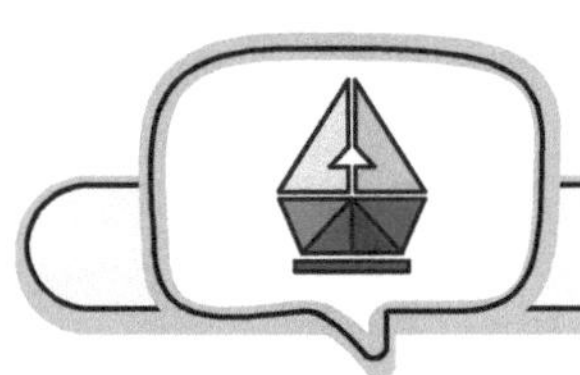

Week 17 • Activity 3

Directions: For each word, circle two other words that relate to it.

Example:

Nighttime

A. sleep **B.** breakfast **C. dark** **D.** sports

1. School

A. learning **B.** yummy **C.** evening **D.** teacher

2. Vacation

A. study **B.** trip **C.** morning **D.** time off

3. Swimming

A. pool **B.** water **C.** orange **D.** dry

4. Art

A. pretty **B.** paint **C.** eating **D.** chairs

5. Concert

A. lunch **B.** music **C.** loud **D.** walking

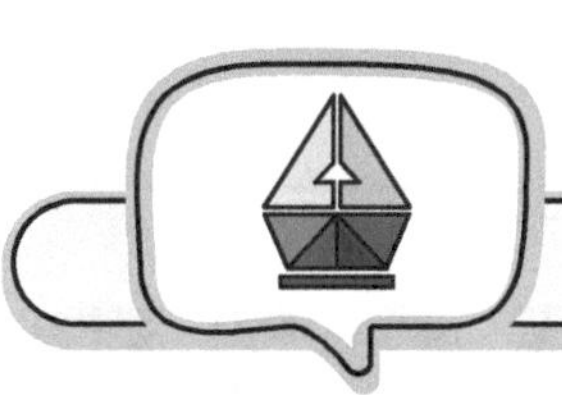

Week 17 • Activity 4

Directions: Write an argument topic, and one sentence that supports your argument with precise, specific words.

Example:

Chocolate chip cookies are the most delicious cookies. They are easy and quick to make, full of chocolate, and tase amazing with a glass of milk.

1. ....

....

....

2. ....

....

....

3. ....

....

....

4. ....

....

....

5. ....

....

....

WEEK 18

Argumentative Writing: Transitions and Conclusions

This week, you'll learn about how to close your argumentative writing in a strong way. A strong argumentative piece is a great tool for convincing people!

Argumentative Writing: Transitions and Conclusions

You've learned how to make strong claims and use reasons and logic in your argumentative writing. Now, you will learn how to link those reasons together and conclude your argument. This includes learning **transitional words**.

Transitional words are words that lead one thought, phrase, or statement into another. There are different types of transitional words. Some are words that show **cause**. Examples of these transitional words are:

because since so

You also use transitional words when moving from one paragraph to another. Transitional words that can be used for this purpose are ones that show the **order** of your thoughts, such as:

firstly next then

There are also transitional words for when you want to talk about **contrast**. This may be a reason the other side of the argument might have, or their counterpoint. These are words like:

but however though

Transitional words for your **conclusion** are special, because they tell the reader you're about to wrap up your argument. You use these words to show that you're finishing your thoughts:

finally lastly in conclusion

Read this section from an example argument, which is about why some people may think crayons are better than colored pencils. The transitions will be <u>underlined</u>. Think about which type of transitional word each one is.

> <u>Firstly</u>, crayons are easier to use than colored pencils. Both crayons and colored pencils let you put color on paper, <u>but</u> colored pencils need to be sharpened. This means crayons are easier to use, <u>because</u> they don't have to be sharpened. This is just one reason why crayons are better.

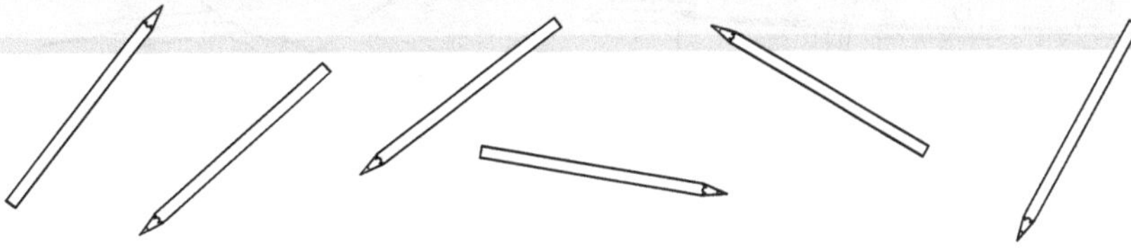

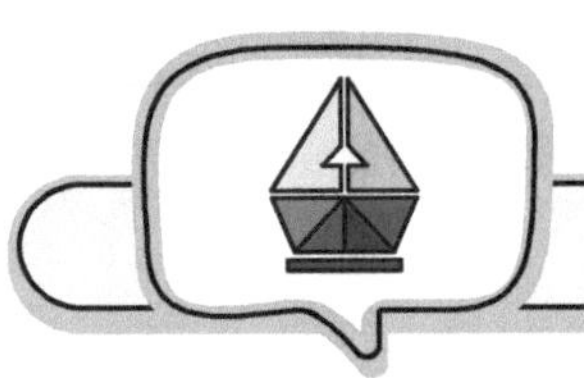

> <u>However</u>, some people might think that colored pencils are better because they have less wax in them, so they won't melt. <u>Though</u> leaving a crayon in the sun may melt it, the crayon can be cooled and work as a crayon again.
>
> <u>Finally</u>, crayons are less expensive than colored pencils. <u>Since</u> crayons are cheaper, it's easier to get a lot of different colors. This means that you can have more color in your drawings, which makes them more fun.

When you're done with your argument, you write a concluding paragraph. This paragraph wraps up all of your thoughts and uses a final statement. This statement should repeat your initial argument in some way. The conclusion does not need to be very long, but it should clearly show your stance on the argument. Here is an example.

> <u>In conclusion</u>, crayons are better than colored pencils. Since they are less expensive and easy to use, they are more fun. Next time you draw a picture, you can use a crayon to see what I mean.

In the activities on the next few pages, you will get to practice identifying and choosing transition words.

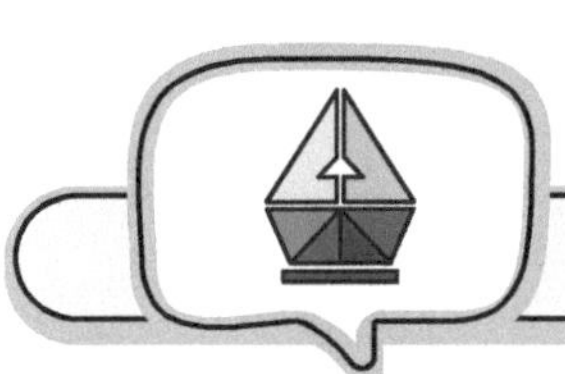

Week 18 • Activity 1

Directions: Use the word bank to identify the transitional word. Write the type of word on the line. You will use each word more than once.

Word bank: cause, order, contrast, conclusion

1. So

2. To conclude

3. In the end

4. Although

5. Additionally

6. While

7. Despite

8. Therefore

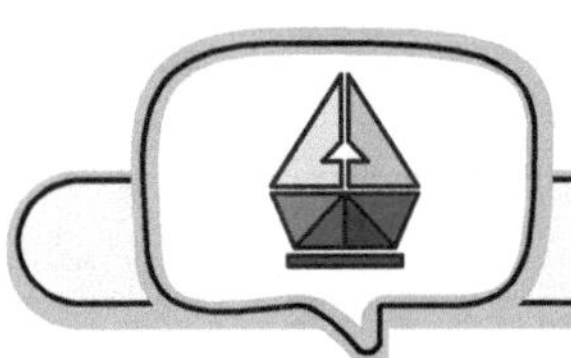

Week 18 • Activity 2

Directions: For each sentence, write a transitional word that shows **cause**.

Word Bank: because, since, so

1. Cats are easier pets .... you don't have to walk them.
2. I ordered chocolate .... it's my favorite.
3. You can be first .... you won last time.
4. She wanted to go, ... I let her in front of me.

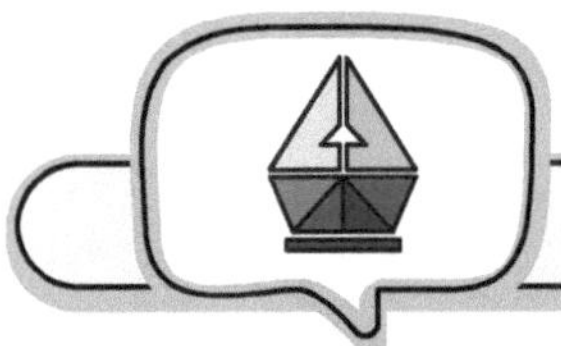

Week 18 • Activity 3

Directions: For each sentence, write a transitional word that shows **order**.

Word Bank: firstly, then, next

1. .... , he already saw that movie, and there's a newer movie out.
2. You like to play soccer, and .... you like to play tennis.
3. The other team should go ....
4. ...., the next chapter starts.

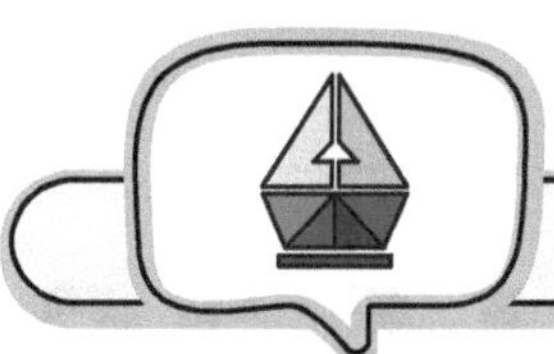

Week 18 • Activity 4

Directions: For each sentence, write a transitional word that shows **contrast**.

Word Bank: but, however, though

1. She thought chocolate was better, ... I like caramel more.
2. .... there were no new books, I bought something anyway.
3. The dog checked its bowl, ... it was empty.
4. I changed the batteries; the new ones were dead, ...

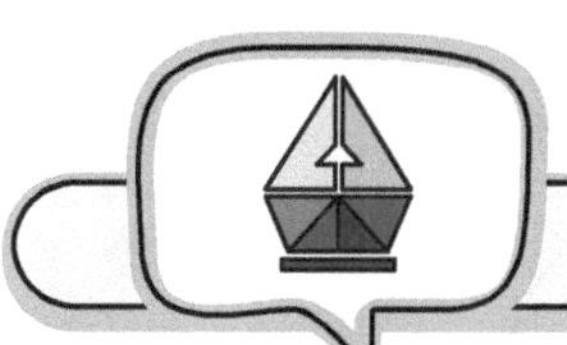

Week 18 • Activity 5

Directions: For each sentence, write a transitional word that shows **conclusion**.

Word Bank: finally, lastly, in conclusion

1. .... , the end of the game was here.
2. I have something I would like to say ....
3. .... , the movie credits rolled.
4. It was fun at first, but I was ...., tired.

WEEK 19

Reading and Writing Poetry

This week we're going to learn about reading and writing three types of poetry - couplets, limericks, and haikus.

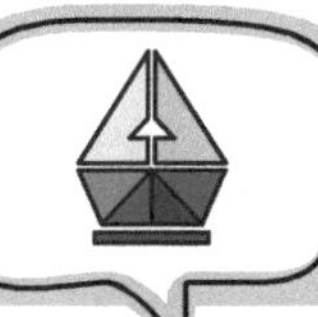

For our final week, we're going to change topics a bit and talk about reading and writing poetry.

Like narrative, informative, and argumentative writing, poetry writing has rules, depending on what type of poetry it is. Knowing the rules for writing poetry can help you read the poetry well, too.

Poetry is a big topic, so we'll only learn about a few types of poems this week. We'll learn about **couplets**, **limericks**, and **haikus**.

Before we talk about the types of poems, let's do a quick review on **rhyming**. Rhyming words are words that sound the same at the end, like "cat" and "bat" or "mop" and "hop". Most poems have a rhyming pattern, or a **rhyme scheme**, and poets use letters to pay attention to which words rhyme. The first set of words that rhyme in a poem are called the **A rhyme**, and the second set of rhyming words are called the **B rhyme**. Read the example of a poem with an AB rhyme pattern below.

A In the moonlight's glow, a playful cat,

A Chases a lively bat.

B Cleaning up the floor with a mop,

B A bunny joins the scene, doing a joyful hop.

Couplets are poems that are two lines long. Couplets always rhyme, and the rhyming words are the last ones in the line. In the couplet below, the rhyming words are underlined.

In twilight's embrace, shadows dance with grace,

Moon whispers secrets to the stars in cosmic space.

Limericks are poems that are five lines long. Their rhyme scheme is AABBA. That means that the first, second, and fifth lines should rhyme, and the third and fourth lines should rhyme. Limericks usually tell a funny story. In the limerick below, the rhyming words are underlined.

There once was a cat named Pat,

Who always wore a stylish hat.

He danced in the sun,

Had so much fun,

That cat in the hat was quite fat!

The last type of poem we'll learn about is a haiku. Unlike couplets and limericks, **haikus** don't have to rhyme! Haikus can rhyme, but the most important rule for a haiku is that it has a certain number of syllables per line. The first line of a haiku has 5 syllables, the second line has 7 syllables, and the last line has 5 syllables. Haikus are usually about nature. Read the example haiku below.

Blossoms gently fall,

Nature's whispers in the breeze,

Spring's silent ballet.

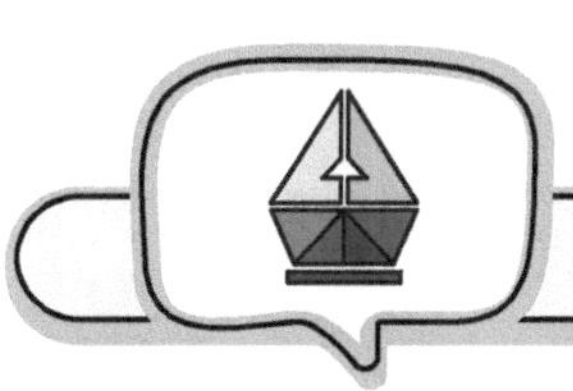

Week 19 • Activity 1

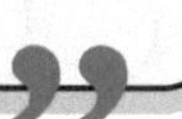

Directions: Use the word bank to write the type of poem on the line. You will use each word more than once.

Word Bank: couplet, haiku, limerick

1. There once was a plane in the sky, Zooming so fast, oh my, oh my! It soared through the blue, With passengers in view, A jet-powered joy, flying high!	**2.** Cocoa warmth swirls, Steam rises in sweet delight, Winter's cozy sip.	**3.** With fur so soft, and eyes so keen, A loyal friend, a canine dream.
4. Ripples in blue grace, Silent strokes beneath the sun, Swimmer's dance in waves.	**5.** In the meadow's hush, where wildflowers sway, Sunset paints the sky in hues of golden ray.	**6.** In space, Laika boldly did roam, A canine astronaut, far from home. With a bark and a cheer, She faced the frontier, Laika's spirit in the cosmos did roam!

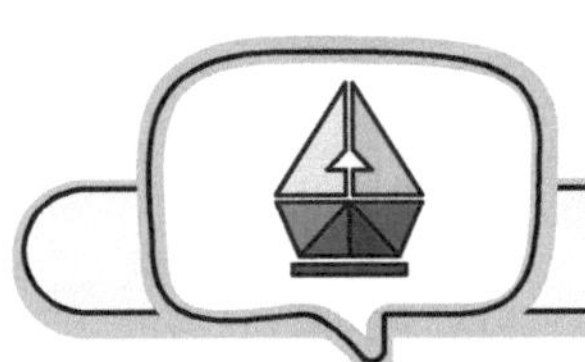

Week 19 • Activity 2

Directions: Finish each couplet poem with your own rhyming words.

1. Cats prowl through the night, silent and sleek,
   In the shadows they roam, mischief they ....

2. Morning sun rises, a breakfast.................................. ,
   Crispy bacon sizzles, eggs sunny-side bright.

3. Engines humming, fast cars take the lead,
   On the open road, a thrilling ....

4. Diamond dreams, a pitcher's bold.................................. ,
   Crack of the bat, into the outfield it'll go.

5. Volcanoes roar with fiery might,
   Earth's restless power, a mesmerizing ....

Now write your own couplet!

....

....

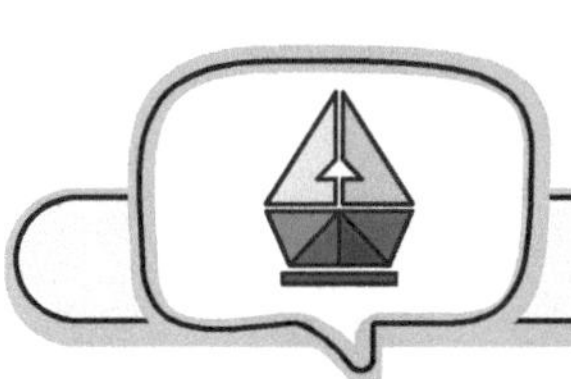

Week 19 • Activity 3

Directions: Finish each limerick with your own rhyming words

1. A playful pup with a wagging .... ,
   Chasing its tail in a joyful trail.
   Barking at squirrels up high in a .... ,
   Furry friend, a bundle of glee,
   In limerick's verse, a dog's tale.

2. In hide and seek, laughter takes the lead,
   Children hide with giggles, a clever deed.
   Counting to ten, the seeker's on a quest,
   Behind curtains or bushes, they ....
   Hide and seek, a game of stealthy .... !

   In a cup, hot chocolate's sweet brew,
   Marshmallows on top, a cozy ....
   Warmth in each sip, winter's delight,
   Cocoa dreams on a chilly .... ,
   Limerick's joy in a chocolaty hue!

   Now, write your own limerick!

   ....

   ....

   ....

   ....

Week 19 • Activity 4

Directions: Write a line for each haiku.

1. ....

   Covered in mist and some trees,

   Nature's perfect art.

2. Pond's lily pad chair,

   Croak echoes in moonlit pond,

   ....

3. Bamboo meal begins,

   ....

   Panda eats a feast.

Now, write your own haiku!

....

....

....

WEEK 20

Review Week

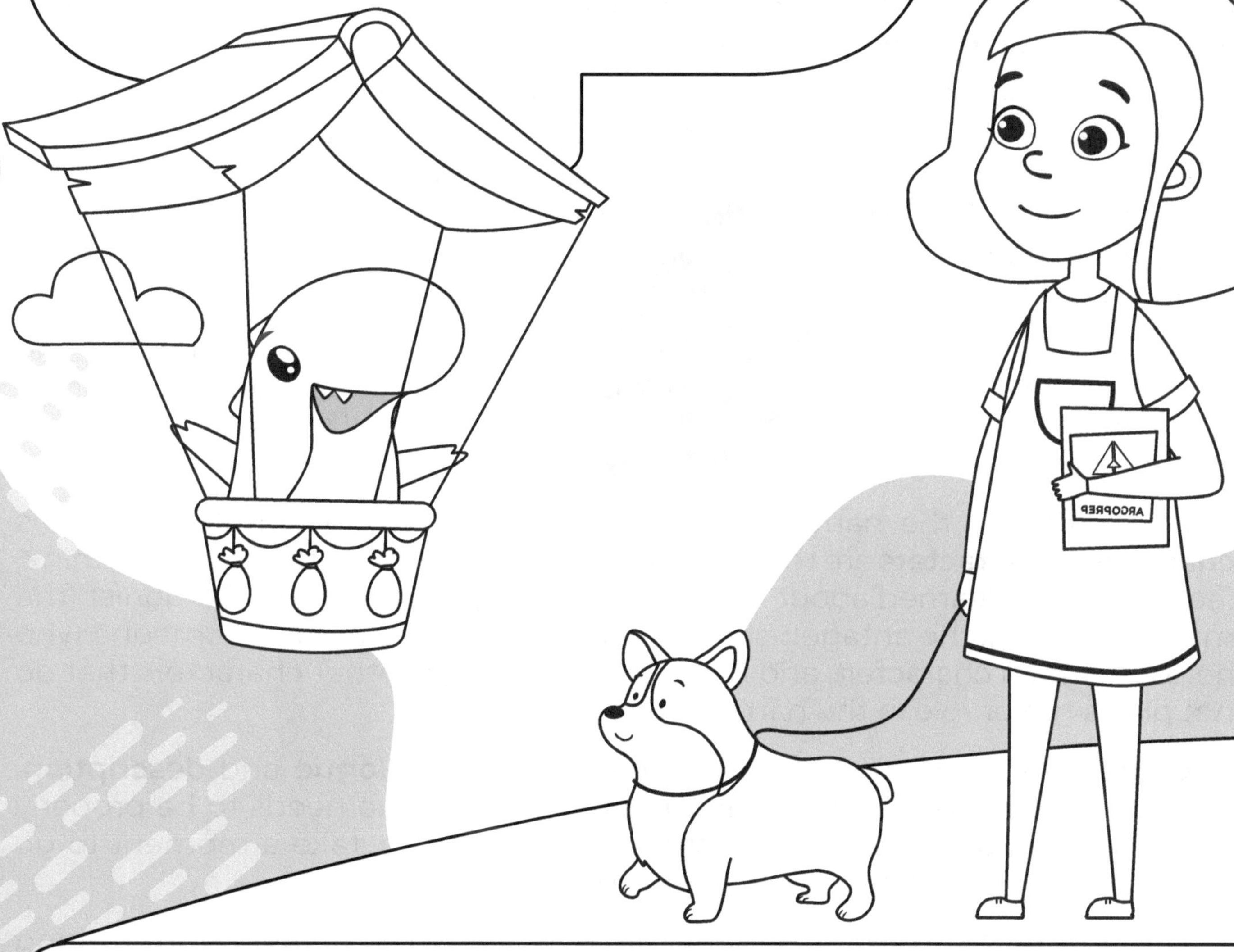

After a lot of hard work, it is time for you to review everything you learned! This week, you'll wrap it all up with a few activities.

Review Week

Way to go! You have finish the whole workbook! This was a lot of tough work, so congratulations on becoming a better speller and writer.

Let's review what you've learned. As you read through this review and do the activities, pay special attention to the lessons that might have been a little bit harder for you. We covered lot of material; it's OK to need to repeat some of the lessons.

In week one, you learned about **similes** and **metaphors**. Both compare two things which may not seem to have much in common at first glance. The difference between the two is **similes** use the words "like" or "as," while **metaphors** say that one thing is the other.

Over the next two weeks, you learned about narrative writing. Specifically, you learned about **narrators** and **characters**, and **dialogue** and **descriptions**. Narrative writing tells a story and the **narrator** is the one who is telling it. The **narrator** can also be a **character** in the story; if this is the case, then it is called a first-person narrative. The story is told through the perspective of the **narrator** as they experienced it.

Sometimes, a writer will choose to write in third-person. If this is the case, the **narrator** is not a **character** in the story, but rather has an omniscient point-of-view. They know everything that is happening and know all of the characters' thoughts and feelings.

In addition to the narrator who tells the story, every narrative contains **characters. Characters** are the people, animals, or things in the story that think, feel, or act. You learned about four major **character** types: the protagonist (the main character), the antagonist (the villain), the deuteragonist (someone who helps the main character), and tertiary characters (all other characters that do not play a major role in the narrative).

Characters come alive for the reader through **dialogue** and **description. Dialogue** is the exact words a **character** says. **Dialogue** needs to be properly punctuated in order to be understood. If you need to, take a moment to go back to Week 3 and review how to write **dialogue**.

Description brings the rest of the story to life for the reader. When writing **description**, focus on trying to make sure the reader experiences the narrative with all five of their senses.

Review Week

Word choice conveys meaning. There are two types of usages -denotative and connotative. Denotative usage is a word's basic, dictionary definition and usage. Connotative usage is how the word is being used in a given context.

Transitional words help to tie ideas together and improve the flow of your writing. **Transitional words** may be a single word or word phrase, like "in conclusion." **Transitional words** can generally be grouped into five categories: time, location, addition, comparison and contrast, and cause and effect.

Concrete words describe real things, things that are tangible and can be experienced with the five senses. **Concrete words** keep writing from being vague and abstract by creating vivid pictures in the reader's mind.

Choosing the right **punctuation** can be just as important as choosing the right words. **Punctuation** divides sentences into various parts and helps make them easy to read and understand. You learned about six different kinds of **punctuation**: full stops (. or ! or ?), commas (,), colons (:), semicolons (;), apostrophes ('), hyphens (-). If you need to take a moment to review how each of these **punctuation** marks are used, do so now.

The last thing you learned about narrative writing was the importance of having a strong **conclusion**. After reading the **conclusion**, the audience should have a clear understanding of why the narrative was written and should feel a sense of satisfaction and completion. There are many different ways to conclude a narrative: summarize the main points, end with a moral, add something personal, share the main character's thoughts and feelings, explain the effect, end with hope for the future.

You also learned about **Greek and Latin root words** and **affixes**. Root words are the building blocks of the English language. They carry the main meaning of the word. **Affixes** are small groups of letters that are added to the beginning or the ending of words to change the words' inflections or meanings.

Over the next four weeks, you learned about **informative writing**. Informative writing is writing that explains, informs, or describes something for the reader. **Informative writing** pieces should have a strong introductory paragraph. The introductory paragraph sets up the topic you are going to talk about. Good introductory paragraphs consist of three parts: an interesting hook that will grab the reader's attention, background information regarding the topic, and a thesis statement.

You also learned that informative writing must contain **facts** and **details.** Supporting **facts** are evidence that proves your point-of-view. Ask yourself, "What **details** will help people understand or believe what I'm saying?" Look for **details** that explain, describe, or give more information about your main idea.

Next, you learned about choosing **content-specific vocabulary**. Content-specific vocabulary words are words and phrases specific to a subject that are rarely used outside of their particular content area.

Finally, you learned about transition words in informative writing.

Transition Words and Phrases	When to Use Them
* In my opinion * She believes * Their favorite	Stating an opinion
* Since * Next * Another reason	Linking ideas or paragraphs
* For example * Additionally * In fact	Providing examples/details
* In conclusion * Finally * To summarize	Coming to a conclusion

You also learned about the conclusion paragraph. The **conclusion** is the final paragraph of the essay. The **conclusion** focuses on the big ideas of the essay, not minor details, and brings everything together.

You took a break from writing to learn about special kinds of words: synonyms and antonyms. **Synonyms** are two words that have a similar meaning to each other, while **antonyms** are two words that mean the opposite of each other.

You then went back to learn about a new type of writing: argumentative writing. **Argumentative writing** is writing that communicates a point of view or opinion to the reader. With argumentative writing, you provide **facts** and **evidence** about your side of the topic. You also learned that word choice is important in argumentative writing, too! Specific word choice helps you **communicate your meaning**. Your last lesson in argumentative writing focused on **transitional words** and **conclusions**.

Transition Words and Phrases	When to Use Them
* Because * Since * So	Showing cause
* Firstly * Next * Then	Showing order
* But * However * Though	Contrasting ideas
* In conclusion * Finally * Lastly	Coming to a conclusion

Then, your last lesson focused on reading and writing poetry. You learned how to read and write three types of poetry: **couplets, limericks,** and **haikus**. You learned that couplets and limericks follow specific **rhyme schemes** while haikus follow a particular syllable pattern.

You've done some amazing work across fourth grade. You are a better writer and speller after all of that hard work. Let's do some activities to further review and practice all that you've learned.

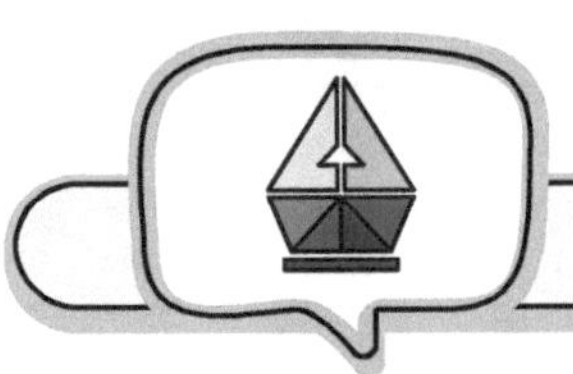

Week 20 • Activity 1

Narrative Writing

Directions: In this activity, you will put together everything you have learned to craft a great narrative writing piece. You may write about whatever you like, but be sure your narrative writing piece includes:

* Characters
* Dialogue
* Descriptions
* Transition words

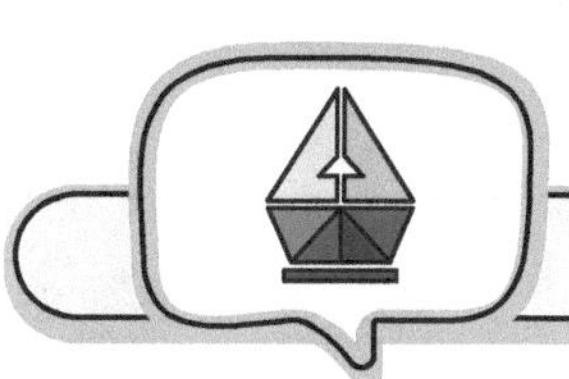

Week 20 • Activity 2

Informative Writing

Directions: In this activity, you will put together everything you have learned to craft a great informative writing piece. You may write about whatever you like, but be sure your informative writing piece includes:

* An introductory paragraph
* Facts and details to teach more about your topic
* Content-specific vocabulary
* Transition words
* A concluding paragraph

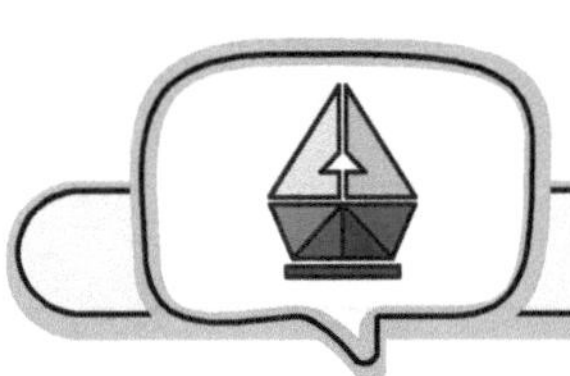

Week 20 • Activity 3

Argumentative Writing

Directions: In this activity, you will put together everything you have learned to craft a great argumentative writing piece. You may write about whatever you like, but be sure your argumentative writing piece includes:

* Facts and evidence
* Specific word choice
* Transition words
* Concluding paragraph

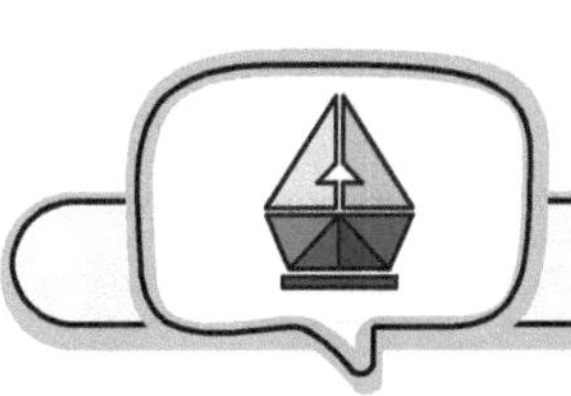

Week 20 • Activity 4

Synonyms and Antonyms

Part 1: Synonyms

Directions: Read each word in the left column. Choose the synonym from the right column that means the same or almost the same thing and write the corresponding letter on the line.

Happy	**a.** Big
Brave	**b.** Difficult
Large	**c.** Sociable
Fast	**d.** Smart
Bright	**e.** Loud
Kind	**f.** Courageous
Noisy	**g.** Nice
Hard	**h.** Quick
Friendly	**i.** Joyful
Clever	**j.** Shiny

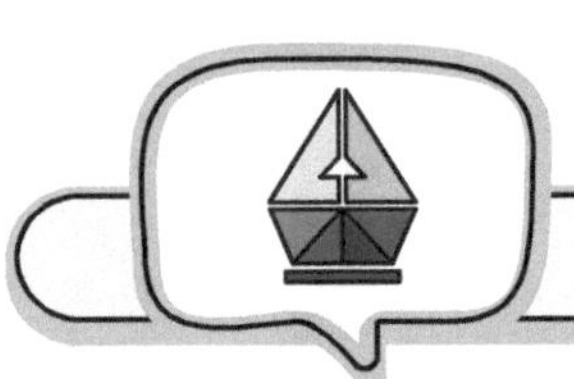

Week 20 • Activity 4

Part 2: Antonyms

Directions: Read each word in the left column. Choose the antonym from the right column that means the opposite and write the corresponding letter on the line.

Hot	**a.** Full
Day	**b.** Far
Empty	**c.** Lose
Win	**d.** Cold
Old	**e.** Sad
Up	**f.** Slow
Happy	**g.** New
Fast	**h.** Down
Light	**i.** Heavy
Near	**j.** Night

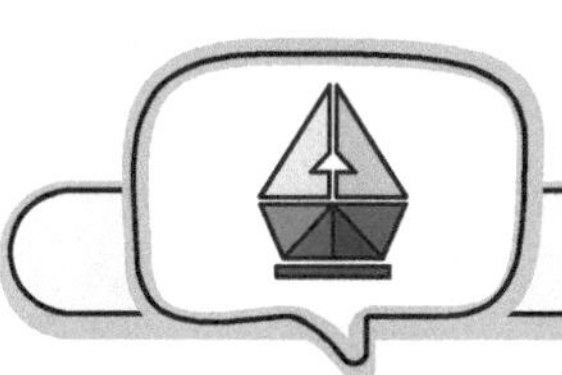

Week 20 • Activity 5

Directions: In this activity, you'll identify each type of poem. Then, you'll write your own! Remember to follow the rules for each poem.

Couplet: AA Rhyme Scheme

Limerick: AABBA Rhyme Scheme

Haiku: 5-7-5 Syllable Scheme

Example Poem	Poem Type	My Poem
There once was a sun in the sky, With a warm and bright gleaming eye. It shone all day long, In a dance, oh so strong, Chasing clouds as they floated on by!		
In sunlit beams, a feline gracefully plays, Whiskers twitch, in the warmth of lazy days.		
Silver night circle Casting shadows, soft and bright, The moon's glow, so nice		

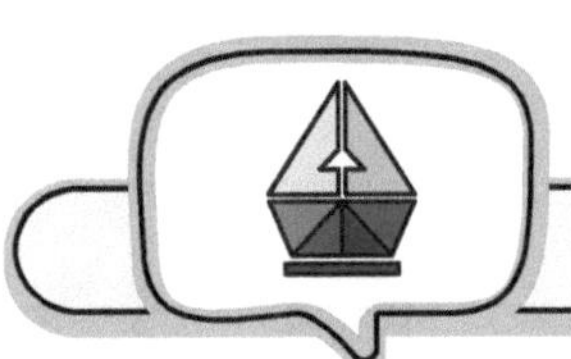

Week 20 • Activity 6

Finding Parts

Directions: In this activity, you will underline the part of the word listed before the word. An example has been done for you.

Example:

Underline the prefix in the word **post**pones.

1. Underline the suffix in the word genetic.

2. Underline the root word in the word inscribes.

3. Underline the prefix in the word understands.

4. Underline the prefix in the word mistake.

5. Underline the suffix in the word relatable.

6. Underline the root word in the word timid.

7. Underline the root word in the word senseless.

8. Underline the suffix in the word business.

9. Underline the prefix in the word substantial.

10. Underline the root word in the word inaudible.

Answer Sheets

To see the answer key to the entire workbook, you can easily download the answer key from our website!

*Due to the high request from parents and teachers, we have removed the answer key from the workbook so you do not need to rip out the answer key while students work on the workbook.

To watch free video explanations go to: **argoprep.com/spelling4**
OR scan the QR Code:

Place your mouse over the workbook you have, and you will see the "Download Answers" button.

For detailed video instructions on how to access the "Answer Sheets," please scan this QR code.

Books explanations

All Books

Grade: 2nd Grade

Series: All

Search...

2nd Grade Common Core Math: Spanish Edition

2nd Grade Introducing Math & Science Workbook

2nd Grade Science: Daily Practice Workbook | 20 Weeks of Fun...

2nd Grade Social Studies: Daily Practice Workbook

Kids Winter Academy by ArgoPrep: Grade 2

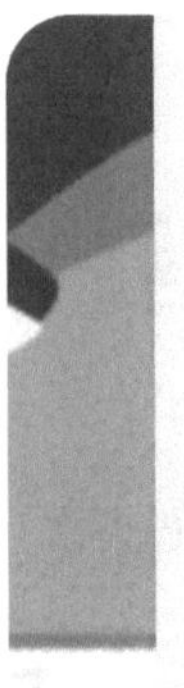

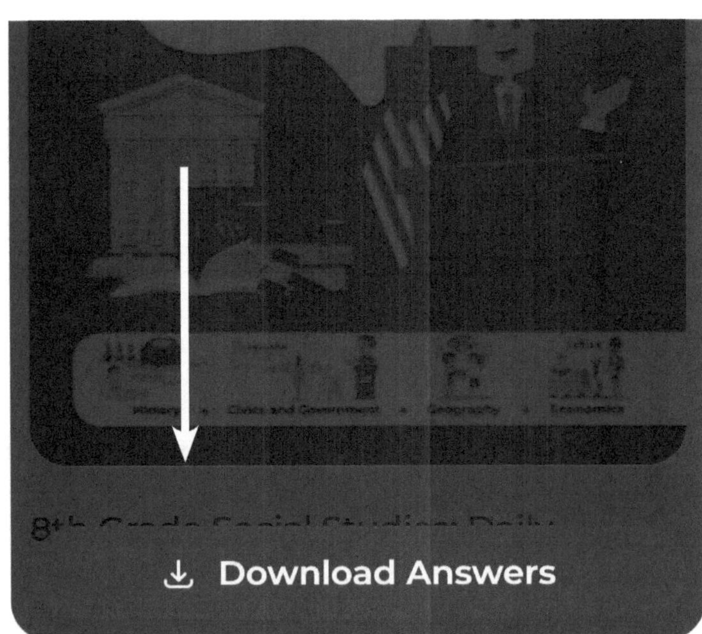

Download Answers

4th Grade Social Studies: Practice Workbook

Made in United States
Troutdale, OR
08/16/2024

22080052R00113